MICHIGAN

in

WORLD WAR II

MICHIGAN

in

WORLD WAR II

DANIEL W. MASON

THE
History
PRESS

Published by The History Press
Charleston, SC
www.historypress.com

First published 2021

Manufactured in the United States

ISBN 9781467147330

Library of Congress Control Number: 2020948660

Notice: The information in this book is true and complete to the best of our knowledge. It is offered without guarantee on the part of the author or The History Press. The author and The History Press disclaim all liability in connection with the use of this book.

A special thank-you to my beloved wife,
who put up with my work on this book the past ten years.

CONTENTS

The Lambda Rho Tau Sorority from Port Huron High School held a fundraiser to raise money for the soldiers during World War II. They posed in the *V* for victory for the men on the front lines. *Photo courtesy of the Port Huron Museum.*

ACKNOWLEDGEMENTS

I thank the following organizations and museums for their help with this book: Algonac Clay Historical Society, Algonac; Allegan Historical Society, Allegan; Alpena County Library, Alpena; Battle Creek Historical Society and Battle Creek Regional Museum, Battle Creek; Bay City Historical Museum, Bay City; Bayliss Public Library, Sault Sainte Marie; Besser Museum, Alpena; Borg Warner Headquarters, Auburn Hills; Byron Center Historical Museum, Byron; Castle Museum, Saginaw; Chippewa County Historical Society, Sault Sainte Marie; Detroit Metropolitan Airport Historical Society, Romulus; Clarington Museum and Archives, Bowmanville, Ontario, Canada; Franklin D. Roosevelt Library, Hyde Park, New York; George H.W. Bush Presidential Library, College Station, Texas; Ernie Harwell Sports Collection, Detroit Public Library, Detroit; Ford Motor Company World Headquarters, Dearborn; Frankenmuth Historical Museum, Frankenmuth; Gerald R. Ford Presidential Library, Ann Arbor; Grosse Ile Historical Society, Grosse Ile; Greenville Military Museum, Greenville; Hamtramck Historical Museum, Hamtramck; Holland Museum, Holland; Hope College, Holland; Icebreaker Mackinac Maritime Museum, Mackinac City; La-Z Boy Museum, Monroe (no longer open); Little Traverse Historical Museum, Petoskey; Los Alamos National Security Research Center, New Mexico; Mackinac Bridge Historical Museum, Mackinac City; Marquette Regional Historical Museum, Marquette; Medal of Honor Museum, Patriots Point, South Carolina, Maxwell Air Force Museum, Montgomery, Alabama; Michigan Military Technology

Museum, Grosse Point; Michigan National Guard, Lansing; Monroe County Museum, Monroe; National Museum of the United States Air Force, Dayton, Ohio; Naval Air Museum, Pensacola, Florida; Oscoda Air Museum, Oscoda; Pennsylvania National Guard Museum, Pennsylvania; Selfridge Military Air Museum, Mount Clemens; St. Ignace Genealogical Society, Saint Ignace; Texas Woman University Library Women Collection, Denton, Texas; Tuskegee Airmen Museum, Detroit; United States Army Corps of Engineers, Sault Sainte Marie; United States Coast Guard Icebreaker Mackinaw WAGB-83 Museum, Mackinaw City; USS *Silversides* Submarine Museum, Muskegon; United States Army Tank and Armaments Command (TACOM), Warren; Walter P. Reuther Library, Wayne State University, Detroit; Waugoshance Lighthouse Preservation Society, Traverse City; Wayne Historical Museum, Wayne WZZM TV, Grand Rapids; and Ypsilanti Historical Society, Ypsilanti.

A special thanks to following individuals for the research they have done on their own points of interest of Michigan during World War II. To a good friend and authority on the Women Auxiliary Ferrying Squadron (WAFS), Sarah Ryrn Rickman, thank you for your help and knowledge of these fantastic women. Thanks also to Kimberly Johnson, archivist and caretaker of the history of the Women Airforce Service Pilots (WASP) at Texas Woman University Library; Brett Stolle from the National Museum United States Air Force; and Bob Kreipke for the photos to tell part of the story of the Ford Motor Company during the war. Kurt Trautman, thank you and your class for recognizing Clarence Zylman in a class project. Thank you, Jef Benedetti, for the donation of your mother's personal effects from World War II to the Detroit Metro Airport Historical Society. I also thank the Heritage Research Center for the list of all of the companies and what they produced before and during the war. Last but not least, thank you Michigan air national guardsman Lieutenant Colonel Brian "Master" Boeding and Patrick Retzer for the history of the 107th Tactical Reconnaissance Squadron during World War II and Rob Sandstrom from the Selfridge Military Air Museum for those photos.

INTRODUCTION

Although most are aware of the bomber factory at Willow Run and the automotive industry's efforts to build military equipment, and though many call Detroit the "Arsenal of Democracy," fewer know that without the small towns in other parts of Michigan, the war might have turned out differently.

A refrigerator company built troop gliders, pleasure boat builders turned their efforts to landing crafts and an auto parts manufacturer shifted to producing gun stalks.

School kids showed their patriotism by raising money for war bonds to buy planes, tanks and jeeps.

POWs worked in our factories, picked crops and cut down trees.

Many well-known people from Michigan served, and others traveled to our state to train for the war.

Many places that were part of Michigan's history during World War II remain, but many others are gone. Probably the most important are the people who served in the military. These men and women fought to keep our freedom and gave the ultimate sacrifice. After the war ended, the count tallied 12,885 men and women from Michigan who died in combat, while training for the war or from injuries after they returned home.

SMALL-TOWN HELP

The automotive industry played a big role in war production, but small-town factories also played a vital role, including the manufacture of nuts and bolts, the mining of raw materials in the Upper Peninsula and the making of socks. Small-town people also raised money to buy war bonds and gave their own earnings to pay for the weapons of war.

After the attack on Pearl Harbor on December 7, 1941, there were rallies across Michigan for young men and women to join the armed forces. On Main Street in Marquette, the high school marching band rallied people to show their patriotism. Instead of waiting to be drafted, men and women enlisted in the branches they wanted to serve. Those unable to enlist because of their age continued to work in the factories, mines and fields for the war effort.

Victory gardens popped up all over the United States. The people of Michigan did their part and grew their own fruit and vegetables. Many food processing companies converted to war production. The Lohrman Seed Company provided a guide to growing victory gardens for people who never gardened before the war.

One of the most unusual things was the call for waste fats from meats. The American Fat Salvage Committee was formed to urge families to save the waste fats used to produce glycerin for explosives. For every pound of fat, it could produce a pound of explosives. Disney Studios even made a film for the public with Minnie Mouse and Pluto explaining how the fats were used.

Photo courtesy of the Marquette Regional Historical Museum.

Photo courtesy of the Marquette Regional Historical Museum.

Photo courtesy of the Marquette Regional Historical Museum and the Battle Creek Historical Society.

It was an effective way to get the public's help. However, as the United States was just exiting the Great Depression, housewives were reluctant to help out for this particular cause.

During war bond drives, captured equipment, such as tanks, trucks, planes and even submarines, was put on display for the public. A Japanese two-man submarine was captured at Pearl Harbor. The occupants somehow lost course, and it was beached. One of the Japanese crewmen was killed. The other member was the first enemy captured and hospitalized. The submarine has been on display in Monroe and Grand Rapids. Holes were cut along the side of the hall so that spectators could see the inside of the submarine. It made its way across the United States to raise war bonds.

One interesting story is about the employees of Universal Engineering Company of Frankenmuth. The company made automotive parts before the war and, like many small companies, transitioned to materials. The employees wanted to do a little bit more and purchased a P-51B Mustang. The plane was named the Spirit of Universal. The employees did not use war bonds to purchase the plane but instead paid with their own money. They raised $50,000.

Left: *Photo courtesy of the Marquette Regional Historical Museum and the Battle Creek Historical Society.*

Below: Oddly enough, as on the side of a milk truck in Marquette, the advertising tells the locals to take the unusable meat to the local school. *Photo courtesy of the Marquette Regional Historical Museum.*

Photo courtesy of the Grand Rapids Public Library.

Before the plane was sent overseas, the United States Army Air Forces painted over the name because of regulations at that time. Universal was able to find out through the War Department where the plane ended up. The employees found out that it was piloted by squadron leader Captain James England, who personalized the plane by having his wife's name painted on the nose.

Universal contacted Jackie England and asked if there was anything they could send to James as a gift. Jackie said that her husband liked cigars. The company then sent eight hundred cigars to the pilot. From 1943 to 1944, England shot down eight Japanese planes. On his last mission with the plane, it sustained thirty-six bullets holes. The army air forces considered that too many and ordered the plane to be scrapped and used for spare parts. Thanks to the ground crew, a piece of the cowl that had the Japanese flags painted on it showing the number of planes shot down was saved. They sent it back to Universal, and it now resides in the Frankenmuth Historical Museum.

Photo courtesy of the Frankenmuth Historical Museum.

In Alpena, the citizens raised enough money to purchase two B-24 Liberator bombers. The city traced both aircrafts and found out that both were shot down. Some of the townspeople even went to Ypsilanti to see what their money bought. There they met some of the women responsible for the construction of these weapons of war. Unlike the pursuit planes, their names were left on the nose of the planes. The people of Alpena did not send any care packages like Universal Engineering Products had, but they did find out that the crew members survived after being shot down.

La-Z-Boy was based in Monroe. When the company moved its manufacturing operations out of Michigan, it set up a new headquarters at another location in Monroe. During the war, La-Z-Boy produced seats for jeeps and tanks. Many vets who returned home after the war probably purchased a La-Z-Boy but were likely unaware that they could have been sitting on one during the war.

The City of Holland sent out invitations to the Crown Princess Juliana of the Netherlands for the Tulip Time Festival in May 1941. Heir to the Dutch throne, she had been living Ontario, Canada, because of the German occupation of the Netherlands. Her husband was serving with

Pilot Captain James England with his ground crewman. *Photo courtesy of the Frankenmuth Historical Museum.*

The piece of the plane that showed the number of Japanese planes shot down. *Photo courtesy of the Frankenmuth Historical Museum.*

The people of Alpena raised money to purchase two B-24 bombers. The first bomber was presented to the military in Alpena. The second was presented at the Willow Run Bomber Plant, and the officials were given a tour of the pant. *Photo courtesy of the Alpena County Library.*

La-Z-Boy's former headquarters in Monroe, Michigan. *Photo courtesy of the Monroe Historical Museum.*

La-Z-Boy employee working on a seat. *Photo courtesy of the Monroe Historical Museum.*

the Royal Air Force in England. Juliana accepted the invitation. This was the only time that royalty visited Holland (Michigan), and in celebration of Hope College's seventy-fifth anniversary, she was presented with an honorary degree.

When the United States began bombing missions over Europe, the likelihood of a bomber crew surviving to complete twenty-five missions was not very good. To improve the morale of the bomber crews in Europe, it was announced that the first plane to complete twenty-five missions would return to the United States to promote the sales of war bonds. The pilot of the Memphis Belle was Captain Robert K. Morgan, and after completing the twenty-five missions, he flew home in the plane on a tour across of the United States. His copilot, Captain J. Verinis, was flying with Morgan in the beginning and completed his twenty-five missions before him. He flew back to the states with Morgan and the Belle. The crew that flew back with them were chosen members who flew with Morgan. The first plane that actually completed twenty-five missions one week before was the B-17 Hell's Angels with a different bomb group.

Opposite: Crown Princess Juliana of the Netherlands accepting honorary doctorate, followed by a dinner reception. *Photos courtesy of Hope College.*

Above: Crew of the Memphis Belle being congratulated on a job well done for completing twenty-five missions. *Photo courtesy of the National Museum of the United States Air Force.*

The name of the Memphis Belle was in honor of Morgan's sweetheart, Margaret Polk, from Memphis, Tennessee. Verinis had seen a movie called *Lady for a Night*, in which the main character owned a riverboat named *Memphis Belle*. He then pitched the name to the crew.

Romulus Army Air Field was one of the stops for the Memphis Belle. A crowd of people turned out to see the famed bomber.

Captain Morgan returned to the war to fly a B-29 Super Fortress in the Pacific. The Belle was on display in Memphis, Tennessee, and fell into disrepair on Mud Island. Morgan was disappointed by its condition and wanted to see the plane brought to the National Air Force Museum, but he passed away before the plane was moved there and restored to its original condition. The plane is now proudly displayed at the National Air Force Museum in Dayton, Ohio.

The Memphis Belle on a war bond tour at Romulus Army Air Field. *Photo courtesy of the Detroit Metro Airport Historical Society.*

Photo courtesy of the Battle Creek Historical Society.

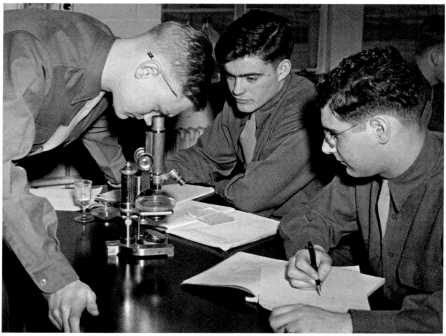

This page: Men engage in military discipline, along with their education. *Photos courtesy of Hope College.*

Taken in 1929 at the Straits of Mackinaw during hunting season. *Photo courtesy of the Mackinaw Bridge Historical Museum.*

Public domain.

Governor Murray Van Wagoner. *Personal collection.*

Kellogg's, of Battle Creek, also helped in the war effort. Before the war began, the army requested individual servings for the men training in the mornings when hot meals could not be provided. Kellogg's continued producing these servings after the war to introduce new products and variety packs for the consumer. Today, there are some small-town diners that still serve individual servings of cereal.

Michigan's colleges and universities helped train our men and women for the war. Doctors and nurses, engineers, translators and many other professions with advanced education were required. Many of these young college students who were military bound were also trained in discipline as officers. It was not unusual for them to be seen marching in line and taking orders, as if they were in boot camp like enlisted men.

When the United States entered World War II, Democrat Murphy Von Wagoner was the thirty-eighth governor of Michigan, and during that time, he encouraged the construction of the Mackinac Bridge. Traveling to the Upper Peninsula created long wait times to cross the Straits of Mackinac by ferry. Construction of the bridge did not begin until 1954 and opened in 1957. There were several ferry lines on both sides of the straits, some of which were operated by the State of Michigan.

PROTECTING OUR BORDERS

Even though the United States was separated from the war by two oceans, our enemies could attack by air and sea. It was evident that Michigan factories were potential targets of air attacks. Japan had aircraft carriers and a secret weapon that was used more for terrorist attacks. Germany was working on long-range bombers and potentially working on long-range rockets. Protecting our borders was so important that even our neighbor Canada assisted.

Before the war, there were four functioning locks on the American side of the border with Canada. In 1941, a railroad bridge collapsed, sending a train engine to the bottom of the channel and killing two men on board. The two newer locks were blocked to shipping. This meant that there were only two locks open, and these were built in the late 1800s. During the war, iron ore mined in the Upper Peninsula and other materials like lumber and grains passed through the locks. Congress had rushed through funding for a replacement lock to be built for increased shipping. In May 1942, ground broke for the MacArthur Lock (named after General Douglas MacArthur). It was completed, ahead of schedule, in 1943.

In Sault Sainte Marie, it was believed that if England lost the war in Europe, Canada would be annexed by the Germans. The FBI believed that the German Luftwaffe could mount an attack from occupied Norway and fly over the North Pole. As the locks played a vital role for shipping, it was imperative to keep them safe from sabotage and aerial attacks. Torpedo netting was drawn across the channel to protect the locks from aerial attacks.

Opposite, top: Two soldiers guarding the Ambassador Bridge from Detroit to Windsor. The American soldier is to the left, and the Canadian soldier is to the right. *Personal collection.*

Opposite, bottom: View over the locks in Sault Sainte Marie. *Photo courtesy of the United States Army Corp of Engineers.*

This page: View of the torpedo netting in front of the lock. *Photos courtesy of the United States Army Corp of Engineers.*

The 131st Infantry Regiment was responsible for defending the locks in various locations, along with several artillery emplacements manned with the 100th Coast Artillery Regiment. With cooperation of the Canadian government, artillery emplacements were stationed in several locations on both sides of the border.

The 339th Barrage Balloon Battalion deployed balloons in the area for defense against aerial attacks. This defense had been used during World War I by the British on the battlefield, as well as in their own country as a guard against aerial attack. Even during World War II, the British continued to use this defense over London. The United States also used balloons on the front line in the Pacific, as well as in the European theater. The balloons were grouped together, making them an obstacle over any potential target, such as the locks. Another early warning signal used to defend the locks was four radar posts in various locations around the region and Canada. An incident occurred when lightning struck six of the balloons, and they caught fire and fell to the river. One of them just happened to land on a roof.

A unit of Black soldiers arrived three months after the United States entered the war to fill the shortage of men for the 100th Artillery Battalion. This was unusual for the community of Sault Sainte Marie, as there was only one Black family living the in the area at the time. Because of racial tensions, the unit was relocated after a year. Some people accused some of the local women of becoming romantically involved with some of the soldiers.

Fort Brady, named after Colonel Hugh Brady, who defended the region from the British during the War of 1812, was located in Sault Sainte Marie. During World War II, there were fifteen thousand men assigned to Fort Brady for the defense of the locks. The fort served as training grounds for harsh weather conditions. The 702nd Military Police Battalion trained for cross-country skiing and replaced the 2nd Infantry guarding the locks. Today, the fort is Lake Superior State University. Many of the buildings still exist.

Many people are unaware that Michigan was attacked by the Japanese. The Japanese had a secret weapon used to demoralize Americans on the home front. The Japanese launched 9,300 bomb-laden balloons that would fly high enough to enter the jet stream and land in the United States. These balloons were called Fu-Go and were designed to drop bombs at a specific altitude to create havoc in the States. The Japanese never found out what havoc they did because the federal government kept this information out of the news. It was the hope of the Japanese that these would take out factories. In many cases, they only caused fires. A family in Oregon died from one of these bombs while out on a picnic in the woods. In Michigan,

Photo courtesy of the Chippewa County Historical Society.

A night of bad weather for a barrage balloon in Sault Sainte Marie. *Photo courtesy of the Chippewa County Historical Society.*

Opposite, top: Member of the 100ᵗʰ Artillery Battalion enjoys some liberty time. *Photo courtesy of the Chippewa County Historical Society*

Opposite, bottom: Behind the men charging is the main barracks. Today it is used as a dorm for the freshmen men. *Photo courtesy of the Chippewa County Historical Society.*

Above: The 702ⁿᵈ Second Military Police Battalion in formation on their skiis. *Photo courtesy of the Chippewa County Historical Society.*

two of these balloons actually landed in Bryon and Farmington Hills. In the Upper Peninsula, the Army Air Forces tried to shoot one down but lost it in the clouds.

The balloon that touched down in Farmington Hills in March 1945 landed in the area of Gill Road and Eight Mile Road. John T. Cook found what he thought was a tin can and tossed it aside in his yard. On June 6, 1945, Cook read in the paper that any suspicious articles found should be turned over to the police. He turned it over to his neighbor Michigan State Police sergeant William Heidt. He found out later that it was a 5-kilogram thermite incendiary bomb from a Fu-Go balloon. The shell would be turned over to army intelligence in Detroit.

On February 23, 1945, three preteen boys spotted an object flying near their home in North Dorr. The three boys, Larry Bailey and brothers Ken and Bob Fein, contacted a family friend, Joe Wolf, to come with his pickup truck and track the object that was coming down near the Feins' farmhouse. They found the balloon on Twenty-First Street, fifty yards from the road. The fabric was flapping in the portion of the balloon that was carrying the bomb, and it ignited, burning the ropes, and the container charred black.

Above: Illustration of the assembly of a Fu-Go balloon. *Photo courtesy of the Chippewa County Historical Society.*

Opposite: *Photo courtesy of the National Museum of the United States Air Force.*

The boys dragged the balloon to the basement of the Feins' farmhouse. The boys asked around to find out what it was, but no one knew. The Fein boys' mother, Genevieve, contacted the family priest, Father Walters. Not knowing what this was himself, he suggested contacting the authorities. Deputies from the Kent County Sheriff's Department thought it might have been a weather balloon that got away, but the weather bureau did not claim it. The sheriff's department then contacted the FBI, which confiscated the balloon. The FBI told the family not to tell anyone what they had found.

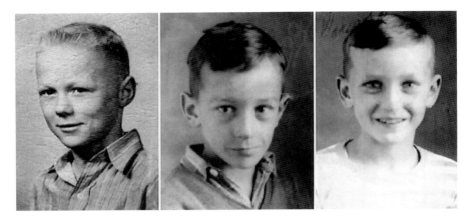

Ben Fein, Ken Fein and Larry Buzz Bailey. *Photo courtesy of Channel 13 WZZM TV, Grand Rapids.*

The story of this balloon doesn't end with the FBI. Don Piccard, serving in the U.S. Navy and assigned to balloon and airship rigging in New Jersey, was tasked with taking care of the recovered Fu-Go balloons. When the war ended, the navy was finished testing the balloons, and the order was given to destroy them. Piccard asked for permission to save one of the balloons for himself. He kept the one from Dorr and would use this balloon to fly in downtown Minneapolis in 1947.

On February 23, 2017, reporter Brent Ashcroft from WZZM 13 out of Grand Rapids did an interview with now retired professor Mike Umsworth from Michigan State University. Umsworth had researched the Fu-Go balloons for decades and showed an article he found in a 2001 issue of *Air and Space Magazine* of Picard's flight over Minneapolis in 1947. Picard was contacted, and it was discovered that he was still in possession of the balloon from Dorr. Theresa Kiel, curator of the Byron Center Museum, contacted Piccard, who was planning to sell the balloon. He was asking $10,000, and an anonymous donor gave the funds for its purchase. The balloon was inflated in June 2017. Members of the museum soon realized that this rare piece of history was too large to put on display in the schoolhouse museum. As of this writing, with the cooperation of the Kalamazoo Air Zoo, plans are afoot to display the balloon there.

Before the war began, the United States Army Air Corps (redesignated the United States Army Air Forces during the war) had several airfields in Michigan where its trained the men in the art of camouflage. The idea was to disguise the plane under tree branches. The outline of a fake plane would then be laid out in another area to deceive the enemy.

Photo courtesy of the Byron Center Museum.

The art of camouflage with a B-25 Mitchell bomber in Alpena. *Personal collection.*

DEADLY DANGER!
HEADQUARTERS
Sault Ste. Marie Military District,
Sault Ste. Marie, Michigan.

March 21, 1942.

TO THE PUBLIC IN: Sault Ste. Marie, Michigan,
Sault Ste. Marie, Ontario.

WARNING!

This District is heavily armed and prepared for instant action. Should we be attacked by air it will only be a matter of minutes before there will be in the air hundreds of heavy-calibre bullets and pieces of large-calibre shells. They will be going up, but a few seconds later they will be falling back.

THEY ARE DEADLY!

Even the bullets can go through the roof of your house. WHEN YOU HEAR ANTI-AIRCRAFT FIRE TAKE SHELTER EXACTLY AS YOU WOULD FROM BOMBS.

FRED T. CRUSE,
Colonel, Field Artillery,
District Commander.

ALGONAC, ST. CLAIR COUNTY, MICH., THURSDAY, JUNE 25, 1942

Algonac's Main Street at Height of Black-out, Sunday, June 21

Above: In Sault Sainte Marie, with the artillery located throughout the city, the commandant from Fort Brady placed an ad in the *Evening News* warning of falling shrapnel from the sky in the event of an aerial attack. *Photo courtesy of the Bayliss Public Library.*

Left: Algonac's local newspaper published on its front page the black square, indicating that the city would not be noticed at night by the enemy airplanes. The locals adhered to making sure that no lights would be seen during a blackout. *Photo courtesy of the Algonac Clay Historical Museum.*

Along with the threats from above, ground threats also hid in plain sight. There was a German spy ring in Detroit. This was discovered after the capture of a German officer in Texas. Two German POWs, Oberleutnant Hans Peter Krug and Oberleutnant Eriche Boehle, had escaped from Internment Camp 30 in Bowmanville, Ontario, Canada. They dressed as Canadian workmen and were escorted by another prisoner dressed as a Canadian soldier, a uniform they obtained from their captors to use in a camp play. They cut through the wires and escaped. A soccer game was arranged that day between the guards and the POWs to serve as a distraction. To fool their captors and the help of fellow POWs, they made papier-mâché dummies, and during roll call, the prisoners would carry them out. They had American and Canadian currency and maps with documentation.

Boehle almost made it to freedom, until he was captured by Niagara Falls Police. The police called the camp commandant and asked him if they were missing prisoners. When the commandants answered in the negative, the police then asked if they had an Eriche Boehle as a prisoner. He was immediately picked up, and because of this, the alert went out for Krug, who was picked up in a San Antonio, Texas hotel room that he had checked into before trying to cross into Mexico.

Krug and Boehle were both given contact names and locations of spies the German military installed before the United States entered the war. Detroit was one of those locations. Krug made his way by stealing a boat and paddling across the Detroit River from Windsor to Belle Isle. There he met with a German immigrant by the name of Mrs. Bertelmann, a pen pal to Krug.

Bertelmann introduced Krug to Max Stephan, a restaurant owner in Detroit and a German spy. Stephan entertained Krug with a tour of Detroit for four days, which included food, beer and even a trip to a brothel. Krug was then set up with a train ticket to Chicago, and from there, he would travel on to Mexico before making his way back to Germany. When Krug was captured and questioned, he told the authorities who helped.

The records of what happened to Bertelmann have been lost. Stephan, however, was brought to trial. He was charged with treason and sentenced to death by hanging. During the trial, he acted like he was unaware what was happening. When the verdict and sentence were read, he proclaimed that Germany would not let him hang and that he would be freed. This was the first time anyone was sentenced to death for spying since George Washington was president. Stephan's sentence was commuted to life imprisonment by President Franklin D. Roosevelt. He died of cancer ten years later.

Above: After overturning this car and setting it on fire, the crowd immediately dispersed when the authorities arrived on the scene of the Mayfair Theater on Woodward Avenue. Many rioters also dispersed when the army released tear gas in the crowd. *Photo courtesy of the Walter P. Reuther Library.*

Left: Oberleutnant Hans Peter Krug waiting to testify at Max Stephan's trial. *Photo courtesy of the Walter P. Reuther Library.*

Left: One of the two dummies used to help in the escape of the German POWs. *Photo courtesy of Clarington Museum and Archive.*

Below: Max Stephan. *Photo courtesy of the Walter P. Reuther Library.*

Not all threats to national security came from without; some dangers were self-inflicted, including the racial tension that was a long-running problem in Detroit. In 1942, many Black people migrated from the South to the northern states for employment, and housing was becoming a problem. The president also made it clear that discrimination would not be tolerated in filling the positions in the factories. Low-income housing was promised for Black people in a housing project called Sojourner Truth. The Detroit Housing Commission wanted to recommission the project for White people and relocate Black people to another area. No other area was acceptable, and the commission was forced to allow the families to move in. A burning cross in a field nearby, believed to be from the KKK, and a picket line of White people tried to prevent the families from moving. These families had already paid their first month's rent and deposits. On February 28, 1942, the day a Black family was to move in, a crowd of around one thousand White people gathered to protest at the intersection of Ryan Road and East Nevada. A riot broke out and lasted for several hours, with dozens of injuries and 108 arrests. There were no other incidents that year, and the Black families settled in the area.

The following year at the Packard Plant, three Black people were placed on the assembly line. The White employees walked off the job in protest. Confrontations began outside the workplace and on Belle Isle. Rumors began that Black women and their children were being abused. Young Black people looted and destroyed property. Then, a rumor about a White woman being murdered resulted in White men beating up Black men near the Roxy Theater as they exited the trolley. The riot began on June 20 and ended on June 23. The Michigan National Guard was called in to control the situation. It ended with 34 dead and 600 injured. Of the 34 dead, 24 were Black, and 17 of them were at the hands of Detroit police, a majority of whom were White. There were 1,800 people arrested, the majority Black.

3

BUILDING SHIPS FOR THE NAVY

The surrounding Great Lakes made Michigan an ideal industrial center. They provided inland ports of safety from German U-boats, and there were many boat and shipbuilders in Michigan. From small pleasure craft to freighters, all of them converted to building military ships, small support boats and other floating craft essential for the navy and, in some cases, the army.

Major Shipbuilders	Cities
American Cruiser	Trenton
Amship Detroit	Detroit
Amship West Bay City	West Bay City
Basic Marine	Escanaba
Chrysler Corp.	Detroit
Dachael-Carter Shipbuilding	Benton Harbor
Davidson Shipbuilding	West Bay City
Defoe Boat and Motor Works	Bay City
Defoe Shipbuilding	Bay City
Detroit Dry Dock	Detroit
Detroit Shipbuilding	Detroit
Great Lakes Engineering	Ecorse
Great Lakes Engineering	St. Clair
Jenks Shipbuilding	Port Huron
Johnston Brothers	Ferrysburg
Wheeler & Co. F.W.	West Bay City

Boat Builders
Chris-Craft
Hacker Boat Co.
Roamer Boat Co.

Cities
Algonac, Cadillac and Holland
Mount Clemens
Holland

Defoe Shipbuilding Company had a unique way of building ships. The hull of the ship was built upside down and, upon completion, would be rolled over on its keel. After the ship was turned, the superstructure and armaments were completed. It was a safe way to build smaller ships, so welders did not have to weld the steel plates above their heads. A couple other shipbuilders were given permission to use this technique to increase war production.

These ships were sent to New Orleans by way of the Mississippi River, except the 220-foot minesweepers and tugs built for the British. Sending the ships down the Mississippi River gave more safety from German U-boats patrolling the Atlantic coast trying to disrupt shipping to England. Out of all the ships that were built, the navy lost only three—one in the Pacific theater by a Japanese suicide boat, one by a German U-boat in the Atlantic and one

Ship launch in the Bay City area. *Personal collection*.

The technique of rolling the ship right side up after construction upside down. *Photo courtesy of the Bay City Historical Museum.*

after D-Day off the shore of Normandy by a mine. The ship could have been saved, but German artillery shelled it, resulting in the loss of ninety-one sailors on board. An additional Defoe-built ship was given to the French navy and was sunk by a German U-boat while on convoy off the coast of Morocco.

In Trenton, Michigan, American Cruiser Inc. built eight submarine chasers. These were wooden vessels about 110 feet long and were very maneuverable. Two ships were sent to our allies on the Lend-Lease Act, one to the Soviet Union and the other to Norway.

It's unknown what happened to the sub-chaser that went to the Soviet Union, but the ship that went to Norway was used in an operation called the Shetlands Bus and was used to transport secret agents and their communication equipment to the Norwegian coast. The spies tracked the movements of the German navy along the Norwegian coast. On the return trips to the Shetland Isles, they would bring important Norwegian personnel and allied airmen to freedom. The ship built in Trenton, the SC-683, was renamed the KNM *Hessa* by the Norwegian navy. While in the war, this ship carried out 114 missions. There was one incident when a Canadian plane mistakenly fired on the *Hessa*. There were no injuries. After the war, the *Hessa* served with the

Top: KMN *Hessa* before it was sent to Norway and designated in Norwegian markings. *Photo courtesy of the United States Naval Air Museum, Pensacola, Florida.*

Bottom: This boat is a Higgins design. *Photo courtesy of the Algonac Clay Historical Society.*

Norwegian coast guard until 1953. After being decommissioned, it was sold to the Sea Scouts and later lost off the coast of Bohuslen.

Originally based in Algonac, Michigan, Chris-Craft produced over ten thousand landing boats. There were two other plants in Cadillac and Holland. At the time, all the boats were built with a marine-grade plywood and were painted to keep an airtight seal. Altogether, they produced over

Above: This type of boat was the design that landed first at Normandy. Note the gun turrets at the bow of the boat allowing a defense on arrival on the beach. *Photos courtesy of the Algonac Clay Historical Society*.

Photo courtesy of the Algonac Clay Historical Museum.

twelve thousand vessels. One little-known fact is that the first boat to hit the beach of Normandy on June 6, 1944, was built by Chris-Craft.

Several of the boats resembled pleasure craft, and after the war, many of the designs were still used for civilian sales. These boats were not just for the navy. They were also used by the army to rescue downed pilots. Chris-Craft ended its Michigan operations in the 1970s and moved to Florida. Today, the plant in Algonac still stands and is a marina for the city of Algonac.

One ship was built not in Michigan but in Toledo, Ohio. It was the USCGC *Mackinaw* WAGB 83 icebreaker. When the United States entered the war, two icebreakers, *Tahoma* and *Escanaba*, were sent to the North Atlantic for escort duty. These small icebreakers kept the shipping lanes on the Great Lakes opened before the war. To keep the shipping lanes open for raw materials from the Upper Peninsula and northern Canada, a larger vessel was needed to clear a passage through the ice.

Congressman Fred Bradley from Rogers City worked toward funding a bill to have a new icebreaker built to handle the job. Other congressmen believed that an ocean icebreaker would be able to do the job without building a new one. The problem was that the drafts of these ocean icebreakers were too large and could not navigate certain parts of the Great Lakes. Senator Prentiss M. Brown from St. Ignace supported Bradley to pass the bill. The construction began in the spring of 1943

Photo courtesy of the United States Coast Guard Icebreaker Mackinaw WAGB-83 Museum.

and the ship was commissioned in December 1944. The *Mackinaw* was originally painted white as camouflage in case of an attack during the winter months. During the time of service on the Great Lakes, its home port was in Cheboygan. After many years of service on the Great Lakes, it was decommissioned in 2005. Today, the USCGS MC83 *Mackinaw* is at a museum in Mackinac City.

4

NAVAL OPERATIONS

T he United States Navy had many different operations in the state of Michigan and the Great Lakes, from administration to training. On the Great Lakes, two aircraft carriers, the USS *Wolverine* and the USS *Sable*, were used for training naval aviators in landings and takeoffs. Both carriers were converted steamship passenger liners used on the Great Lakes. These carriers were shorter than those used in combat. Since the Great Lakes were more inland, they provided more security for pilot training. The planes they used were combat-weary and expendable if the training pilot had to bail out or crashed.

The USS *Wolverine* was a passenger liner built in Wyandotte, Michigan. It had over 510 staterooms and held 1,500 passengers. On the Great Lakes, it was known as the *Great Ship See and Bee*, for *c* and *b*, the initials of the company that owned the ship, the Cleveland and Buffalo Transit Company. The *Sable* was also a passenger ship on the Great Lakes that went by the name *City of Buffalo*. In 1939, the company that owned the ship filed for bankruptcy, and the ship was purchased by V.J. McGuire, who sold the two ships to the U.S. Navy a year later. The *Great Ship See and Bee* and the *City of Buffalo* were refitted, the passenger quarters above the hull of both the ships were removed and the flat deck was placed on top. The smokestacks and bridge were moved off to the side to have the full deck for landings and takeoffs on both ships. By 1942, the *See and Bee* was recommissioned as the USS *Wolverine* (IX-64). Both ships had over 170,000 successful takeoffs and landings.

Public domain.

The USS *Sable* (IX-65) in port at Chicago during the winter months. *Photo courtesy of the United States Naval Air Museum Pensacola, Florida.*

Right: *Personal collection.*

Below: Re-creation of the plane sitting on the bottom of Lake Michigan at the United States Naval Academy. *Photo courtesy of the United States Naval Air Museum Pensacola, Florida.*

Photo courtesy of the United States Naval Air Museum Pensacola, Florida.

About 250 training planes rest at the bottom of the Great Lakes. One plane raised from Lake Michigan is now in the Kalamazoo Air Zoo Museum and is a Dauntless dive bomber. The pilot ditched the plane because he thought he had run out of fuel. When the plane was raised, it was discovered there was still fuel in the reserve tank and oil in the engine.

One plane recently recovered from Lake Michigan saw combat in the Battle of Midway. This plane is on display at the Naval Museum in Pensacola, Florida, in the condition it was in at the bottom of Lake Michigan. The navy still owns the planes and museums that wish to have one for their collection need to prove they have enough funding to raise the plane and to restore it for static display. Once recovered from the bottom of the lake, the plane is sent to Pensacola for restoration before going to the museum funding the recovery.

The *Sable* was also tasked with a secret project near Traverse City. The navy was looking for ways to save more lives with unmanned aircraft. The project was called STAG-1 (Special Task Air Group One). An aircraft was built around RCA's early television. RCA's top scientist, Dr. Vladimir Zworykin, was the designer of this project. The aircraft was designed and built by Interstate Aircraft. The camera was mounted in the nose of the

Above: Displayed on the open nose of the drone is a view of the camera. *Photo courtesy of the United States Naval Air Museum, Pensacola, Florida.*

Left: View of a pilot with the removable cockpit. An example of the drone is on display hanging from the ceiling of the Naval Air Museum. *Photo courtesy of the United States Naval Air Museum, Pensacola, Florida.*

Photo courtesy of the Waugoshance Lighthouse Preservation Society.

plane, and a person was in another plane to pilot. The pilot would be in a TBM-1C Avenger watching with a five-inch screen and guiding the plane to potential targets. These drones, known as TDR-1, could carry a one-thousand-pound bomb or a torpedo.

The navy ordered two thousand of these aircrafts but took only two hundred of them. The rest of the order was canceled. These planes were tested out in the Traverse City area. Fifty of the planes saw combat, and thirty-one of them destroyed their targets. The targets were antiaircraft sites, bridges, airfields and grounded ships. These planes never took off from an aircraft carrier in the Pacific. Admiral Halsey did not want them on his carriers, even though the planes were ferried to the island base by carrier. The project had ended by October 1944, because the United States had gained air superiority over Japan.

In 1851, the Waugoshance Lighthouse was built in the Mackinac Straits. This was to replace a lightship in this shallow, difficult-to-navigate area of Lake Michigan. By 1912, the lighthouse was decommissioned when ships with deeper drafts started using a deeper channel along the straits. The

British Airmen class photo at Grosse Naval Air Station. *Photo courtesy of the Grosse Ile Historical Society.*

Tombstones of the fallen RAF (Royal Air Force) pilots in a local cemetery in southeast Michigan. *Personal collection.*

lighthouse was used in this experiment to show what kind of damage the TDR-1 could do. The drones dropped bombs and was flown directly into the lighthouse. Today, all that remains is the shell of the lighthouse, with the pipes of the foghorn. At the time of this writing, the Waugoshance Lighthouse Preservation Society is raising money to restore the lighthouse.

The U.S. Navy had facilities throughout Michigan, from Traverse City to Grosse Ile. The base at Grosse Ile, which just borders Canada, was a training base for pilots. Before the war, it was a reserve base and handled many amphibian aircraft and a dirigible.

England and Canada both sent young pilots to train to fly at the naval base before the United States' entry to World War II, an attempt to protect them from being shot down by the Germans. The constant air raids over England made it difficult for the English to train their pilots during the Battle of Britain, with the German fighters shooting them down. Many naval aviators trained beside the British and Canadians. Some of these pilots were so welcomed during the war that they returned to live in the surrounding communities after the war. Some of them were invited into the local homes for dinner and enjoyed homemade meals. Some of these pilots died in training accidents. Because of British military traditions, their remains are buried where they died serving their country. Their remains are here at two local cemeteries in Flat Rock and Trenton.

Before he became the host of several game shows on television, Bob Barker was a young ensign training at the Grosse Ille Naval Base. He was fortunate enough to not see combat in the Pacific, because Japan surrendered after he completed his training. He was quoted in his biography, saying, "The Japanese heard I was coming and decided to surrender."

5

MICHIGAN NATIONAL GUARD

Michigan had several National Guard units called to active service before and during the war. Some of these units have the distinction of being the oldest in the United States military, dating to the War of 1812. One unit was performing reconnaissance along the French coastline. Another was in the Pacific theater fighting the Japanese in the jungles of New Guinea. One battalion was involved with the Battle of the Bulge. Congress honored these men after the war for their heroism.

The 107th Aero Squadron formed during World War I. After the First World War, it was demobilized until it was reorganized by the State of Michigan as a National Guard unit and operated out of a garage in Detroit. The state had changed the designation to the 107th Observation Squadron and supplied them with $2,000 to refurbish each plane that the Army Air Corps had supplied them. These were surplus planes that were being retired. The 107th called itself the Red Devils. The squadron would eventually be relocated to a new facility at Wayne County Airport when it opened in September 1930.

It wasn't until 1940 that the squadron was called to active service. Its job was to patrol the East Coast, spot German U-boats and take photos of their movements.

In 1943, the squadron was transferred to England, where it changed designation again to the 107th Tactical Reconnaissance squadron. When the members first arrived in England, their planes did not arrive with them, and the Royal Air Force supplied the squadron with British Spitfires. Eventually,

Photo courtesy of Selfridge Military Air Museum.

When deployed on the East Coast, the planes used were the Douglas O-38 biplane and the Douglas O-47. *Photo courtesy of Selfridge Military Air Museum.*

Pilot and ground crew in Europe with the P-51B Mustang. *Photo courtesy of Selfridge Military Air Museum.*

the squadron changed over to the P-51B Mustang. Its job again was taking photos of the enemy and their movements. The 107th played a key role leading up to D-Day. The squadron was responsible for all of the photos of the beaches at Normandy for the landing craft and the drop zones for our paratroopers in the invasion of France. It was given a presidential citation for this work. On D-Day, the squadron gave close ground support to the 1st Army. One mission the squadron had was locating a German airfield that had captured American planes. There were bombers and fighters who were shot down, and the Germans were repairing them. They would use these planes to infiltrate Allied squadrons flying over Germany and fire on the Allied planes from the squadron.

The Thirty-Second Infantry, known as the Red Arrow Division, comprised Michigan and Wisconsin National Guardsmen. They were mobilized in 1940 and were going to be sent to Northern Ireland but were instead sent to Australia in May 1942. Elements would be sent to New Guinea to fend off a potential invasion from the Japanese. They arrived in November 1942 and met the enemy in Buna, New Guinea. This was the first troop movement of

Left: *Public domain*.

Below: Portrait of the national guardsmen in the Pacific Theater. *Courtesy of the Fort Custer Historical Museum.*

One of the many bridges the 254th Combat Engineer Battalion assisted in constructing. *Photo courtesy of the Library of Congress.*

the war for the United States. This would be the most difficult battle they would endure. Shortages of medicine and food and the extreme heat and humidity of the jungle made many men sick with fever. The Japanese fought to the last man at every position the Thirty-Second took. In total, 1,954 men lost their lives fighting, and another 2,952 died of disease. After Buna, the Thirty-Second moved on the Philippines and saw more heavy fighting in Luzon and Leyte.

The Thirty-Second Infantry holds the record for continuous combat with the enemy for more than a year and a half. Six of the members received the Congressional Medal of Honor. The division also received a Presidential Unit Citation for its combat record.

A platoon from the 254th Combat Engineer Battalion also played a key role on D-Day. They were among the troops in the first wave landing on Omaha Beach in Normandy, clearing mines and repairing roads and bridges to break the defenses of the Germans. The 254th helped provide the link up to Utah and Omaha beachheads combing the Allied forces. The rest of the men in the battalion who were from the Upper Peninsula arrived on June 8, 1944.

The 254th took part in the race across France and was one of the first units to enter Paris, building bridges and removing obstacles and mines.

Photo courtesy of the Library of Congress.

In September 1944, it accompanied the 5th Armored Division to reach the German lines. It destroyed fifty-two German fortifications along the Siegfried Line. It was involved in five campaigns and received a Presidential Unit Citation for the members' heroism during the Battle of the Bulge. During the battle, they were reassigned to infantry to defend the lines against the heavily armored Germans. They held off the first two attacks against the Germans, until they had to retreat because of German artillery. They held off the Germans for over nine hours, until relieved. The engineers later took part in constructing the longest tactical bridge in the war across the Rhine River.

6

WE CAN DO IT

With men going off to war, women stepped up to fill in the positions the men used to have.

Women also enlisted in the armed forces. The Women's Army Corps (WAC) and Women Accepted for Volunteer Emergency Services (WAVES) handled clerical work and communications, such as switchboard operation, telegraphs and other duties that could relieve a man to go to the front lines. Perhaps the most skilled were the women who had experience flying aircraft. These women were known as WAFS (Women Auxiliary Ferrying Squadron). They ferried aircraft from coast to coast from factories and airfields. Later, these WAFS became part of a larger organization and were called the WASP (Women Airforce Service Pilots), towing targets, transport and testing aircraft.

The song by Kay Kyser called "Rosie the Riveter" was about the women working in the factories, so the women who worked in the factories were known as "Rosies." One poster showed a muscular woman dressed in coveralls having lunch on the job. Another is the iconic image showing a woman with her sleeves rolled up and making a fist, reading, "We Can Do It." While appearing in a promotional film at the Willow Run bomber plant in Ypsilanti, Michigan, actor Walter Pidgeon discovered that there was a riveter named Rose. Rose Will Monroe was born in Somerset, Kentucky, with nine brothers and sisters. She grew up as a tomboy and worked with tools. When her husband died in a car accident, she found work at the plant to take care of her family.

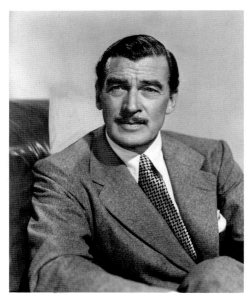

Left: Walter Pigeon. *Personal collection. Right*: Rose Monroe. *Photo courtesy of the Ypsilanti Historical Museum.*

Pidgeon asked Rose Monroe to appear in a promotional film to raise war bonds for the government. Though she agreed, Rose never capitalized on the fact that she appeared in the film. She continued to work even after the war, driving a cab and working in a beauty salon. She also founded Rose Builders, a construction firm that specialized in homes. She passed away in June 1977 in Clarksville, Indiana.

Women had to support their families while their husbands went off to war. Ford Motor Company hired many women to work the assembly lines, including the Willow Run Bomber Plant in Ypsilanti. Some of the women who were more petite had the job of working inside the wings when riveting the metal skin on the plane. Other women worked with machinery.

Some of the women who could not work in the factories found other ways to help. Those with seamstress skills made sweaters for the servicemen. Some made parachutes or sewed fabric on aircraft parts, such as ailerons, rudders and flaps. The women of Rockford Bowling League proudly held up a quilt with the embroidered names of the people who bought raffle tickets for a chance to win it. The money raised from this patriotic red, white and blue quilt came to $211.44 to help purchase a plane for the War Department.

Women worked in many different jobs to take the place of men. Some worked with machinery, while others continued to work clerical positions.

Above: *Photo courtesy of Ford Motor Company.*

Right: *Photo courtesy of the Ypsilanti Historical Museum.*

Above: *Photo courtesy of the Ypsilanti Historical Museum.*

Opposite, top: Rockford Bowling League. *Photo courtesy of the Rockford Historical Museum.*

Opposite, bottom: These women are working on parachutes at the Nash-Kelvinator plant in Grand Rapids. *Photo courtesy of the Grand Rapids Public Library.*

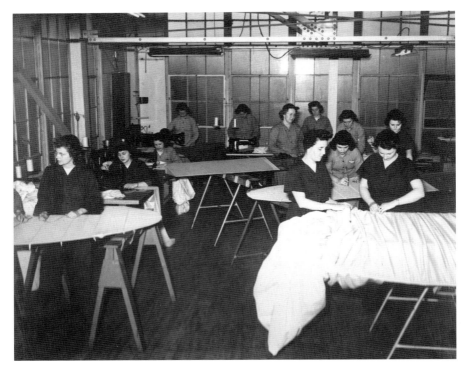

WAVES sewing new fabric to wings at Grosse Naval Air Station. *Photo courtesy of the Grosse Isle Historical Society.*

There were also women who enlisted with the armed forces to handle positions men normally did. Some women were flight instructors, and some assisted with the training equipment, such as a Link trainer used to help pilots learn to fly planes by just the instruments in the cockpit. These ladies were members of the WACS (Women Auxiliary Corps), in which women joined the U.S. Army to fill positions that would relieve men needed on the frontlines. The only difference between WACS and the WASP is that these women were given military status and benefits after the war.

Black women were also accepted in the army. Like Black men in the army, it was common for women to be discriminated against, but they persisted and did their part.

The U.S. Navy had several installations in Michigan and on the Great Lakes, with its own women volunteers called the WAVES. This organization was established by Congress in the summer of 1942 and was signed by Franklin D. Roosevelt. This new reserve of the navy lasted six months after the war. These women did clerical work and sewed

Private Marilyn Wheaton giving instructions to Private Eileen Atkinson on the operations of the link trainer at Romulus Army Air Field. *Photo courtesy of the Detroit Metro Airport Historical Society.*

Black women enter the mess hall for a meal at Fort Custer. *Personal collection.*

fabric to aircraft wings and other parts of the planes that were damaged in training.

During World War II, Detroit Metro Airport was called Romulus Army Air Field, and there were 107 WAFS assigned from January 1943 until December 20, 1944. Adela Riek Scharr was one of the first five WAFS assigned to Romulus Army Airfield. The commanding officer, Colonel Carlyle Nelson, saw the potential of using these women and sent Adela and Barbara Donahue for advanced training in the P-39 Airacobra pursuit plane. Both ladies finished top of the class because they did something the men did not: they read the flight manual on the aircraft.

These women flew trainers, pursuits and other twin-engine planes. They were respected by the men and showed that they were just as capable of handling the aircraft. They flew the P-39 Airacobra and the P-63 Kingcrobra from Buffalo, New York, to Romulus and then to Great Falls, Montana. The planes were flown on to Alaska and then the Soviet Union on the Lend-Lease Act. The Russians were using these planes for close ground support, taking out German tanks with the 37mm gun in the nose of the plane. These planes had the engine located behind the cockpit and a drive shaft for the propeller. This allowed more fire power in the nose for a 37mm gun that ran through the center of the propeller and two 50mm caliber machine gun and the guns in the wings.

Of the 1,109 women who served with the WASP, only three were minorities: a Native American woman and two Asian American women. Black women were not eligible to fly, though Black men were given the chance. One of the Asian American pilots, Hazel Ah Ying Lee, was assigned to Romulus Army Airfield. Her parents were immigrants from China, and she was born in the United States. She learned to fly before the war, and when Japan attacked China, she wanted to join the Chinese air force. Because she was a woman, the Chinese military would not allow her to fly. To help China, she did what she could by buying planes, supplies and anything else that she could for her parents' native country.

When the opportunity came to use her talents to fly for the United States, she didn't hesitate. When she was assigned to Romulus, she was also trained to fly pursuit planes, the P-51 Mustang, P-39 Airacobra and the P-63 Kingcobra. While flying into Great Falls, Montana, her plane was in the same flight path as another. The controller tried to communicate with both planes, but it was too late. Hazel was pulled from the wreckage severely burned. She died a few days later. Not too long before her death, her brother was killed in action in Europe while serving with the U.S. Tank Corps. Her

Left: Adela Riek Scharr. Before the war, she was the first woman in St. Louis, Missouri, to receive her commercial pilots license. *Photo courtesy of Texas Woman University*.

Below: WASPs (*left to right*): Mary Darling, Margaret Kerr and Margaret Ann Hamilton. They are standing in front of a P39 Airacobra that was ferried from Buffalo, New York, to Romulus, Michigan, to Great Falls, Montana. *Photo courtesy of the Detroit Metro Airport Historical Society*.

Hazel Ah Ying Lee. *Photo courtesy of the Detroit Metro Airport Historical Society.*

parents found a nice location in Portland, Oregon, on a sloping hill looking over the Willamette River at the River View Cemetery. They went to court to have them buried there because the cemetery had a policy that only White people could be buried at that location, but the family prevailed. Hazel was one of thirty-eight women who lost their lives serving with WASP. In 2004, she was inducted to the Oregon Aviation Hall of Fame.

7

SCHOOLKIDS SHOW
THEIR PATRIOTISM

To show their support for the war effort, many schoolkids found ways to raise money. They took part in scrap drives. Many wrote letters to family serving in the war. These kids had fathers and mothers, big brothers and big sisters and aunts and uncles who were involved in the military and wanted to do what they could for the cause. Every little thing they did made a difference.

Greenville students raised money to purchase troop gliders from Gibson Refrigerator Co. The students raised $7.2 million to purchase four gliders. On March 19, 1943, the students christened one the Fighting Falcon at a ceremony at Black Field, in which General Harold "Hap" Arnold announced to the residents that this glider would be the first to land in the invasion of Europe. The students received the coveted Distinguished Service Award from the U.S. Treasury Department—the first time in history a group of students earned the award.

Lieutenant Colonel Mike Murphy was a special friend of General Arnold. Murphy volunteered to fly the glider, even though he was a B-17 pilot. Many gliders were designed to carry a jeep and troops. This glider was not and was modified with a metal plate to hold a jeep, making the plane heavier than if it held only troops. First Lieutenant John L. May was the copilot. General Donald F. Pratt, with his aide, had his personal jeep lashed down with radio equipment and five containers of gasoline.

After a two-and-a-half-hour tow trip to the drop zone in an unstable glider, Murphy released the tow line and proceeded to land the glider. Because

Gliders lined up in the Gibson Refrigerator plant in Greenville, Michigan. *Photo courtesy of the Fighting Falcon Military Museum.*

this was an early morning landing, Murphy and May could not know that the moist night air had made the field slippery. Murphy was unable to stop the glider on the ground and it slid into a row of trees. General Pratt was seated in the passenger seat of the jeep wearing his steel helmet, and his aide sat in a jump seat behind the jeep. Colonel Murphy found himself hanging halfway out the glider still strapped to his seat and wearing his steel helmet. General Pratt and Lieutenant May were killed on impact, and the aide was miraculously uninjured but stunned. Murphy was flung through the windshield and broke his legs. This was depicted in the Steven Spielberg movie *Saving Private Ryan*, but in the film, the pilot is up walking and directing men and the glider also carries troops.

Colonel Murphy had to play dead while German troops passed. He had to wait most of the night, until a medic arrived with morphine. It's unknown what happened to the other three gliders the students purchased for the army. Several gliders have been reproduced with the Fighting Falcon label, including one in the Fighting Falcon Military Museum in Greenville, Michigan.

(*Left to right*) General's aide, General Donald E. Pratt, Lieutenant Colonel Mike Murphy and First Lieutenant John L. May. *Photo courtesy of the Fighting Falcon Military Museum.*

After the glider crashed, a photo was taken of a GI holding the skin of the glider to show the Falcon name. *Photo courtesy of the National Museum of the United States Air Force.*

Like many other communities, Hamtramck citizens allowed the children to take part in scrap drives, collecting materials as diverse as paper and tin cans. Everything was recycled for the war effort. Rubber tires were needed because the rubber supply from Asia was cut off. In Hamtramck, two local parishes competed to raise the most scrap metal and, in both cases, had a car in the pile of metal. It started with the kids from St. Ladislaus School making a pile at their playground, and the kids from St. Florian felt they could do better. A teacher from Pilsudski School, Jeannie Kedsierski, contacted the parents of her students to save all their tin cans by removing the lids and flattening them for collection.

Japan occupied many countries in the Pacific, and one of the materials needed to make life preservers was a cotton fiber called kapok from the pods of a ceiba tree. Dr. Boris Berkman, a Russian immigrant from Chicago, had been working with milkweed pods and the fibers inside them. Berkman found twenty different uses of milkweed, and one of them was as a replacement for kapok. He worked with the U.S. Navy and found that 10 pounds of this material could keep a 150-pound man afloat in the water for forty hours. A sum of $250,000 was granted to build a plant to manufacture these life preservers. Along the shores of Lake Michigan, Petoskey seemed to be an ideal location

Kids sit on top of the newspaper that was collected. *Photo courtesy of the Hamtramck Historical Museum.*

Photo courtesy of the Hamtramck Historical Museum.

Jeannie Kedsierski with some of her students. *Photo courtesy of the Hamtramck Historical Museum.*

Left: Dr. Boris Berkman. *Photos courtesy of the Little Traverse Historical Society.*

Bundles of milkweed pods hanging to dry out. *Photo courtesy of the Little Traverse Historical Society.*

Some of the Alpena kids, who picked more milkweed than the surrounding communities. *Photo courtesy of the Alpena Public Library.*

Kids in the Petoskey area picking milkweed pods in a field. *Photo courtesy of the Little Traverse Historical Museum.*

Dedication of the B-17 Flying Fortress that was purchased by the students of Grand Rapids. *Photo courtesy of Grand Rapids Public Library.*

for all modes of shipping and for the abundance of milkweed growing in the region. In fact, there were drying stations throughout the region before the pods were brought to the factory.

Throughout the Midwest, children picked the milkweed pods to raise money for different organizations. The money was not much, but it helped organizations like the Red Cross and the USO. The children of Alpena made it a competition with other communities in the region to see who could collect the most milkweed, and they proved that they could.

The students of South High School in Grand Rapids raised $75,000 to buy a pursuit plane for the Army Air Forces. They were so ambitious that instead of $75,000, it became $300,000, after which buying a B-17 Flying Fortress was a better choice. The kids raised another $75,000, and in April 1943, the plane was flown into Kent County Airport for a christening ceremony. The plane was named the Spirit of South High Grand Rapids, Michigan. The original cost for the planes was only $340,000, and the remaining $35,000 was used by the government for the war effort.

8

MICHIGAN AVIATION

Before the war, there were a few companies, such as Ford Motor Company, building planes throughout Michigan. Some of the companies just built components during the war, while others were able to get contracts to build small planes. The aircraft industry was still in its infancy, and the war forced improvements on building aircraft designs and capabilities. The automotive industry played a major role in the mass production of aircraft with its assembly line techniques.

Eddie Stinson, founder of Stinson Aircraft Company, had two plants in Northville and a third plant in Wayne. Today, all that is left of the plants is the machine shop and some of the runway, which is located at the **GM Engine** plant in Romulus. Stinson died in an air crash in Chicago in 1932 while on a sales trip. The company was bought by several companies and was owned by Consolidated Vultee before World War II. During the war, the British Royal Navy and the U.S. Army purchased the proven L-5 Sentinel and the AT-19/V-77 Reliant. These planes were used for training and close artillery spotting, medical evacuation, reconnaissance and passenger transport. The L-5 was known as the jeep of the skies. Many of these planes were test flown to Grand Rapids, where they were taken apart and crated up and sent to the frontlines. The company was fortunate to build these aircraft. Some of the smaller companies only had contracts to build other precision products, such as aerial cameras.

Employees of the Stinson Aircraft Company. *Photo courtesy of the Wayne Historical Museum.*

AT-19/V-77 Reliant. *Photo courtesy of the Wayne Historical Museum.*

L-5 Sentinel. *Photo courtesy of the Wayne Historical Museum.*

In Ypsilanti, Ford Motor Company was contracted to build components for Douglas Aircraft and then assemble an aircraft designed by Consolidated Aircraft. The plant construction began in 1940 and was completed in 1942. Problems with parts that they were receiving appeared to be an issue, and Ford got permission to build a complete B-24 Liberator bomber. Every part would be produced in-plant. Willow Run comprised the plant, two hangars, an airfield and housing for the employees. An expressway was built from Detroit to the plant so that the employees did not have to live in the area.

The hangar was used to change parts in the planes that did not pass quality control and in the event that a part was changed during production for upgrade or defect. A rail that runs around the top of these structures was believed to be for blackout curtains to keep production continuing in case of an air raid. No known photo has been found to prove the actual function, but like many of the Ford plants, there was a tunnel system between the buildings that could have been used during an air raid.

Across the United States, factories found ways to recycle every piece of scrap metal. Ford even found a way to retrieve the bullets from the sand pit

This page: From the Willow Run Bomber Plant. *Photos courtesy of the Ypsilanti Historical Museum.*

The sand pit where the guns from the B-24 were tested. *Photo courtesy of the Ypsilanti Historical Museum.*

used to test the machine guns on the B-24 Liberator bomber. A powerful magnet was used to pull the spent bullets from the sand pile. The bullets were melted and used again to make more bullets or some other part.

The Willow Run Bomber Plant had built 8,645 planes by the time it ended production at the end of the war. Of those 8,645 planes, 1,893 were

Above: Photo courtesy of the Ypsilanti Historical Museum.

Opposite: The last disassembled B-24 Liberator fuselage in a shipping container. *Photo courtesy of the Ypsilanti Historical Museum.*

put in crates and shipped to the frontlines, where they were reassembled. After the war, the plant was repurposed several times, building planes and then automobiles and eventually changing hands to General Motors to produce transmissions.

A portion of the plant saved from the wrecking ball will be a museum housing aircraft and telling the history of the Arsenal of Democracy.

9

THEY TRAINED IN MICHIGAN

The Selective Service Act passed by Congress in 1940 prohibited racial discrimination in the armed forces. As a result, the army established flight training at the Tuskegee Institute in Alabama. There, Black pilots trained to fly for the Army Air Forces. One of those men was Benjamin O. Davis Jr., who would eventually rise to the rank of general after the war. The Ninety-Ninth Fighter Squadron was the first trained and was sent to French Morocco in 1943. Though trained in flight, the Tuskegee Airmen never received any aerial combat training before they were sent into combat and basically had to learn on their own, with occasional tips from White pilots.

The next group that learned to fly was sent to Selfridge Airfield. The pilots did not remain long and were moved to Oscoda Airfield in May 1943, along with the group headquarters. In Oscoda, the pilots learned gunnery and combat training, as well as discipline as an officer.

One of the most intriguing pilots among the Tuskegee Airman was Lieutenant Walter J.A. Palmer. When he heard of a football game between the Tuskegee Institute football team and State College, a Black educational institution in Detroit, he decided to make a flyby over the field. The first time he flew at five hundred feet above the football field and then decided to fly lower so that the spectators could see it was a Black pilot. He did this a third time to show the crowd that the Tuskegee pilots were doing fine by flying at the level of the stands. This allowed the audience to see him do a slow roll as he pulled up.

Photo courtesy of the Selfridge Military Air Museum.

Unfortunately for him, Colonel Robert Selway was attending the game. Selway ordered a court martial for Palmer but later rescinded it because fellow pilots and instructors vouched for his talents as one of their best pilots. Instead, Palmer was docked three months' pay (seventy-five dollars a month).

Another stunt Lieutenant Palmer did was to fly under the Blue Water Bridge in Port Huron. He did this at night to test his skills. Alexander Jefferson had also flown under the Blue Water Bridge and said that if you were not scared doing this, you were just dumb. Growing up in the Detroit area, Alexander learned to fly before the war, and when the opportunity came along to fly pursuit planes, he enlisted.

Alexander was shot down and become a POW. When the camp was liberated at the end of the war, he was asked if he was aware of the concentration camp down the road in nearby Dachau. He and a friend walked to see what their liberators were talking about and witnessed the carnage of the Nazi's ultimate plan of genocide.

The navy was not the only group that lost planes in the Great Lakes; the Army Air Forces also lost a few. While training in Michigan, some of the Tuskegee lost planes in Lake Huron and Lake St. Clair. In fact, a few Tuskegee Airmen lost their lives during their training. Some of these planes have been found and documented by a marine archeologist, Wayne

Left: Lieutenant Walter J.L. Palmer. *Right*: Alexander Jefferson. *Photos courtesy of Maxwell Air Force Museum.*

Blue Water Bridge joining Port Huron, Michigan, and Sarnia, Ontario, Canada. *Photo courtesy of the Port Huron Historical Museum.*

Alexander Jefferson in his retirement years standing in front of his uniform at the Tuskegee Museum in Detroit. *Personal collection.*

Lusardi, with the Department of National Resources at the Thunder Bay National Marine Sanctuary. One such plane found was a P-39G Airocobra that was flown by Tuskegee Airman Lieutenant Moody, whose body washed ashore after he crashed. Wayne had assembled a group of volunteers to help with the documentation of the site. The group was called "Diving with a Purpose." Ernie Franklin asked after the dive who the pilot was and found out it was an airman who graduated from Tuskegee with his math teacher Richard Macon from Detroit High School.

Not everyone at the Tuskegee Institute was trained to fly. Those who did not pass flight school had the opportunity to be aircraft mechanics and trained in Oscoda and then Selfridge Field near Detroit. These men did an exceptional job of maintaining the aircraft for the Tuskegee Airmen. Every aircraft mechanic considered that the plane was theirs and that the pilots were just borrowing them.

In 1944, a new 477th Bombardment Group was formed to add more bomber squadrons in the Pacific theater. This was doomed to failure, because Colonel Robert Selway, commanding officer, was a strong proponent of segregation. He made conditions unbearable, attempting to force these men to quit. The group did not remain at Selfridge for training and was

Wayne Lusardi and Ernie Franklin preparing to lay a wreath on the water in honor of Lieutenant Moody. *Photo courtesy of Wayne Lusardi.*

The wreckage of Lieutenant Moody's P-39G at the bottom of Thunder Bay. *Photo courtesy of Wayne Lusardi.*

Photo courtesy of Selfridge Military Air Museum.

transferred many times, until it ended up at Freeman Field in Seymour, Indiana. It was at this field that the 477th faced mutiny charges for an attempt to integrate an all-White officers club. One of Detroit's own played a role in these events.

At every airfield where Selway was in command of Black troops, he did not allow them to take advantage of the officers club. Even though the military was to be nondiscriminatory, Selway's orders were enforced. Eventually, this caught up to him, and he was disciplined.

One of Detroit's former mayors, Coleman A. Young, was a Tuskegee Airman who trained with the 477th. Most people knew Young for his politics first as state senator and later as mayor of Detroit. In his autobiography, he told of his time as a Tuskegee Airman. At first, he tried to avoid being drafted because of health issues, but the military doctors still approved him for duty. He was first sent to Fort Custer, training in the infantry. He and his brother went in together, but during a long march cross-country, his brother had to be carried because of arthritis. His brother was later transferred, but not discharged, because of this medical problem.

Young rose through the ranks from private to sergeant. When the opportunity came along to sign up for officers' training school, he jumped at the chance. He was assigned to a military police unit that would handle Black soldiers who got into trouble. He wrote a poem about the discrimination of the Black officers, which made its way to the commanding officer in charge, who figured it had to be written by an educated Black man. Young felt fortunate that the commander did not figure out it was him.

All 101 Black officers were flown to Godman Field on charges of mutiny and were confined to one location fenced in on base. Since these men were officers, they had orderlies to shine their shoes and take care of their laundry. Many of the orderlies would bring information about what was happening. Eventually, the charges of mutiny were dropped, except for three. Two of the officers were acquitted, and one of the three was docked fifty dollars a month for three months as punishment. General Hunter, the commanding officer, and Colonel Selway were transferred out. Word had it the now

Photo courtesy of the National Museum of the United States Air Force.

Left: *Personal collection.*

Below: Young (*third from the right*) with some of the arrested officers at Freeman Field, Indiana. *Photo courtesy of the Tuskegee Air Museum Detroit Chapter.*

promoted General Benjamin O. Davis Jr. was to take command, and Davis knew of Young's role in the mutiny. Young had to decide whether to resign from the Army Air Forces or transfer for more training. He took the latter choice and trained as a celestial navigator. As he was leaving the base, Young passed Davis and saluted him.

Making his way to Selman Field, Coleman Young arrived to continue his training, but the war had come to an end with the bombing of Hiroshima and Nagasaki. The Black officers took advantage of entering the officers club again at night, at which point most of the White officers were already inebriated. The commanding officer even offered Young a glass of champagne. The next morning, after realizing what had happened and sobering up, the commander gave the Black officers the choice of reenlisting for another eighteen months or resigning their commissions and taking a discharge. Young took the discharge.

The Tuskegee Airmen had trained at Oscoda Airfield for nine months, and it wasn't long after that training began for another group of airmen. French freedom fighters were in exile from France during the war, and some of them trained at Selfridge, as well as Oscoda. The infrastructure was already in place after the Tuskegee Airmen were transferred out of Oscoda. General Charles de Gaulle, leader of the French army, also paid a visit to the French airmen to check on their training.

General Giraud served in both world wars and was captured by the enemy in both. In World War I, he was captured in 1914 and escaped by pretending he was part of a traveling circus. In World War II, he was captured in Belgium while in command of the Seventh Army in defense of the German invasion in 1940. He was imprisoned in Königstein Castle for high-security POWs near Dresden. He was court-martialed for the order of the execution of two German saboteurs. Wearing civilian clothes, he again escaped his captors.

It took him over two years to make a rope out twine, torn bedsheets and copper wire. He escaped by climbing down the side of a cliff of the mountain fortress. As a disguise, he shaved off his mustache and wore a hat. He made it to Switzerland, a neutral country throughout the war. He eventually made it back to France and made it clear to the Vichy government that he would not cooperate with Germany.

Heinrich Himmler had ordered the Gestapo to assassinate Giraud and to capture any of his family to discourage him from working with the Allies. He was secretly contacted by the Allies and given the name "Kingpin." He agreed to help the Allies with the invasion of North Africa, provided that it

Opposite, top: General Giraud exiting a plane at Romulus Army Air Field to inspect a plane. *Photo courtesy of the Detroit Metro Airport Historical Association.*

Opposite, bottom: Flight Officer Gene Autry with RAF pilot. *Photo courtesy of Jef Benedetti, from his mother, Solange DeHooghe.*

Above: Texan T-6 trainers lined up on the field with British RAF markings. *Photo courtesy of the Detroit Metro Airport Historical Society.*

would be with only the Americans. He had no respect for the British after the retreat from Dunkirk. Giraud wanted France to keep its sovereignty, and President Roosevelt agreed.

The British and Canadians pilots were not restricted to Grosse Ile; they trained in other parts of the country and occasionally stopped at Romulus Army Airfield. A story in a local paper, the *News Herald*, stated that some of the British pilots returned to southeast Michigan after the war. One of the stories was that while they were training at Grosse Ile Naval Base, they would follow the railroad tracks south for some distance before returning to base. The army pilots who were flying the B-24 Liberator bombers south would fly above the same tracks. Because of the rivalry between the army and navy, the bomber pilots would fly low enough to make the turbulence rough for these young British and Canadian pilots.

10

HOLLYWOOD COMES
TO MICHIGAN

What better way to inspire the communities of Michigan than celebrities attending events across the state? From war bond drives, golf outings, parades and USO shows for the troops who were training in Michigan to simple factory appearances for a tour and talking with the employees, these stars played their part.

Many people are aware of Gene Autry's service to our country during the war. Gene could not sit idle when war broke. He wanted to be a fighter pilot and, because of his age, was turned down by all branches, except for the Air Transport Command. Basically, it said that he could still serve and fly but not fighters or bombers. He became a flight officer and flew needed supplies to our troops in unarmed cargo planes.

He flew the China-Burma-Indonesia run over the mountains. He could have been shot at any time. He also continued his radio show for the Armed Forces Radio, but after his first tour of duty, he was sent back to the United States as Flight Officer Gene Autry. This was a noncommissioned officer position that was equivalent to the rank of master sergeant. Gene was sent to Luke Field, but by March 1945, he was sent to Romulus Army Airfield (now Detroit Metropolitan Wayne County Airport). While stationed at Romulus Airfield, Gene toured Michigan and performed for the troops. He also encouraged women to join the WACS and interviewed a few potential women.

Phyllis Ada Driver was born in Lima, Ohio, in 1917. She studied at Sherwood Music Conservatory in Chicago for three years, but never having

Gene entertained at a local dance hall in Wayne, Michigan, and would also entertain at the airfield in the officers' club.
Photo courtesy of Jef Benedetti, from his mother, Solange DeHooghe.

confidence as a musician, she changed careers. Phyllis transferred to Bluffton College in Ohio, where she handled humorous editorials.

Phyllis married Sherwood Anderson Diller at the age of twenty-two, and they had six children. She worked as an advertising copywriter. When the war came along, Sherwood found work at the Willow Run Bomber Plant, and the family moved to Ypsilanti. Phyllis helped raise her family while she worked as an accountant on the side. On weekends, she did standup comedy at the Tap Room in Ypsilanti, delivering one-liner housewife jokes, and played the organ for the church choir on Sundays.

Phyllis's career did not take off until after the war, when her family moved to California, where she performed her comedy act in 1955 at San Francisco's Purple Onion nightclub. Phyllis divorced Sherwood in 1965 when her show business career took off.

Bud Abbott and Lou Costello were the biggest comedy team in Hollywood during the war. Like many celebrities, they toured the United States to help in the war bond drives. Together, the pair raised over $85 million—more than any other Hollywood celebrity. They passed through

Above: Sonja Henie, Olympic gold figure skater, stopped by the Grosse Ile Naval Base to rally up the service men and women. *Photo courtesy of the Grosse Ile Historical Society.*

Left: Phyllis returned to Ypsilanti years later to visit the friends she left behind after the war. *Personal collection.*

Michigan, visiting several cities like Hamtramck and Marquette in the Upper Peninsula.

It came at a cost to Costello. One day, he had to perform a comedy skit on the radio. He told his only son that he could stay up to listen to him on the radio for the first time, but later during the day, his son was taking a nap. The nanny took advantage of this to rest herself. His son woke up and wandered

Opposite: James Cagney chatting with a contributor. *Photos courtesy of the Hamtramck Historical Museum.*

This page: Bing Crosby taking a swing at the golf outing fundraiser. *Photo courtesy from the Grand Rapids Public Library.*

out to the pool and fell in and drowned. Costello was informed of this and still performed his act. The audience did not know until after the show, when Abbott came and announced what had happened. His close friend Maxene Anglyn Andrew, one of the members of the Andrew Sisters, said Lou was never the same after that.

James Cagney appeared in a war bond rally in Grand Rapids and mingled with the locals. During the war, Cagney appeared in the lead role in *Yankee Doodle Dandy*, which is about songwriter, actor and director George M. Cohan's life and the patriotic songs he wrote during World War I. Bing Crosby, a passionate golfer, showed up for a golf tournament to raise funds for the war effort. When the war broke out, thirty-eight-year-old Crosby registered for the draft. He did not serve but did spend twenty-five weeks performing for the men while also performing on radio shows.

11

POWs

You might have heard of German POWs in your hometown during the war. The Geneva Convention, established after World War I, outlawed hard labor. With many young White men away fighting in the war, this left too many jobs open for women, migrant workers and Black men to fill. So, German and Italian POWs were given the option to work in the farm fields, lumber camps and food processing factories to earn money and buy items from the camp store. There was one high-ranking German officer who resigned his commission to go to work and earn money. The general was so well liked by the civilians he worked with that it was believed that if he escaped, he could have been helped by the locals. When the army looked at his status in the community, he was not allowed to do any more work outside the camp.

Devoted Nazis brought to Fort Custer tried to enforce the discipline of the German army on other German prisoners. Many POWs who did not comply would have been beaten or possibly killed. These men were weeded out at Fort Custer and sent out of state to camps in Alabama and Oklahoma. The camp in Oklahoma was considered the "Devil's Island" of camps because of its security.

There were escape attempts by the Germans in a few of the camps. Because of the Geneva Convention, these POWs eventually returned to their own countries after the war, though many Germans and Italians came back and became citizens through sponsors and marrying Americans.

Above: Camp Allegan. *Photo courtesy of the Allegan Historical Museum.*

Below: POWs demonstrating their woodworking skills. *Personal collection.*

Opposite: Camp commandant observing some of the POWs crafts. *Photo courtesy from the Marquette Regional Historical Museum.*

Camp Allegan, located in Allegan County, had around 250 POWs, and many of them volunteered to work in the fields to earn money to spend at the camp store. While working in the Heinz factory in Holland, Michigan, some of the prisoners were so amazed by the onion peeler that Heinz donated one to the camp.

There was an escape attempted, but the prisoner did not get far. He thought that Lake Allegan was Lake Michigan and decided to make an escape by swimming to the other side, thinking it was Wisconsin. The guards met the POW on the other side of the lake and brought him back to the camp. The prisoner had the right idea, but it was a matter of geography and not understanding how large Lake Michigan is.

With little to do for entertainment, some of the Germans used their spare time woodworking. There were six POW camps in the Upper Peninsula, where the Germans were not a problem. There were escape attempts, and on one occasion, the owner of a motel rental was informed that there were three escaped POWs. When he returned to his motel, he came across the three. He invited them in to warm up since it was fall and very cold outside. He offered them food and beverage and called the police. They arrived, and the POWs were picked up without incident.

Many of the guards who were at these camps were older than the soldiers overseas. They never had problems with the prisoners. Many of the prisoners expressed that they liked the United States, and if Germany won the war, they would move to the States. Camp Germfask in the Upper Peninsula was the only POW camp that held conscientious objectors. These were Americans who refused to fight in the war because of their religious beliefs, and many of them were troublemakers. Many of the prisoners refused to go on work detail because they were not part of the military. They made life miserable for the guards.

There were a few escape attempts, one of which was not really an escape attempt but just a case of someone left behind while out on a work detail. When it was realized that one of the POWs was missing, the guards went back to the work site and found him walking along the road on his way back to camp.

Officers were exempt from working because of their rank. Many of the enlisted soldiers had jobs outside the camps but none related to war production. They worked picking crops and plants, like the Heinz plant in Holland, Michigan. In the Upper Peninsula, they worked in lumber camps. They would buy beer and cigarettes at the end of the day and socialize. The PX was a place where the prisoners had a chance to socialize with the guards and other Americans.

POWs enjoying beverages they were able to purchase with the money they earned.
Personal collection.

Other POWs who were being held in the United States were Italians. At the beginning of the war, Italy was an ally of Germany, and the two countries fought together in Africa. Some of the captured Italians were sent to the United States to be held in POW camps. In Michigan, some of them were held at the state fair grounds and Fort Wayne in Detroit. Toward the end of the war, the Italian people overthrew their leader, Benito Mussolini, and surrendered to the Americans. The Italian POWs were given the opportunity to either remain prisoners or work until the end of the war. Many of them chose to work and were free to explore the city of Detroit. Some of them met their future wives, and at the end of the war, the women went to Italy. One of the Italians had cooked for the army, and when he returned to the United States after the war, he ended up opening his own restaurant in East Detroit. His family stills operates the restaurant, along with two others.

Though there are many enemy combatants buried throughout the United States from World War II, Fort Custer National Cemetery is the only cemetery where soldiers' remains from an enemy country are laid to

Italian POWs working in the mess hall at Fort Wayne. *Photo courtesy from the Walter P. Reuther Library.*

rest. Sixteen German POWs were out on a work detail with their guards when the truck carrying them and the guards was struck by a train. They were laid to rest at a cemetery at Fort Custer, along with ten other German prisoners who died of natural causes. When the war ended, the military made the grounds a national cemetery for our fallen soldiers and veterans. The German graves remained and are marked on the grounds where they are located.

During the summer of 1941, Japan prevented one hundred Americans from returning to the United States. President Franklin D. Roosevelt approached the State Department on how to handle this problem. John David Dingell Sr. was on the Ways and Means Committee and made a recommendation to keep Japan from creating any more trouble. Until Japan allowed the Americans to return home, Dingell suggested that for every American held in Japan, one hundred people of Japanese ancestry and Japanese people in the United States with visas be held in one location in America. John's letter was sent to the president in August 1941.

The Germans were able to have ceremonies for their departed comrades. *Photo courtesy of the Fort Custer Museum.*

There are twenty-six Germans laid to rest at the Fort Custer National Cemetery, some of whom died of natural causes. *Photo courtesy of the Fort Custer Museum.*

FROM 1943 TO 1946, FORT CUSTER HOUSED GERMAN PRISONERS OF WAR. A TRUCK/TRAIN COLLISION RESULTED IN THE DEATHS OF SOME OF THE 26 GERMAN SOLDIERS BURIED HERE. OTHERS DIED OF NATURAL CAUSES SINCE 1953. GERMAN AMERICAN COMMUNITIES AND VETERANS ORGANIZATIONS HAVE SPONSORED AN ANNUAL MEMORIAL SERVICE TO HONOR THOSE WHO ARE RESTING HERE.

DEDICATED: VOLKSTRAUERTAG 1991
YOUR GERMAN AND AMERICAN FRIENDS

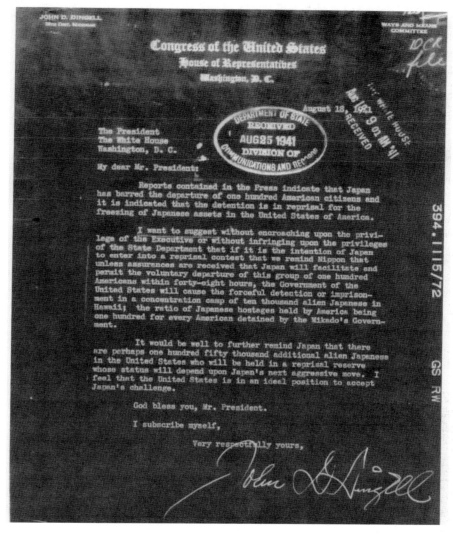

Opposite, top: All of the German soldiers have tombstones, and family members may visit the site of their graves any time. *Personal collection.*

Opposite, middle: U.S. representative from Michigan John Dingell Sr. *Personal collection.*

Opposite, bottom: John David Dingell Sr. served in Congress for the twelfth district of Michigan from 1933 until his death in 1955. He was an advocate for universal health care. *Personal collection.*

Above: *Photo of letter courtesy of the Franklin Delano Roosevelt Library.*

After the attack on Pearl Harbor, Roosevelt signed Executive Order 9066, intending to prevent espionage on American soil. This was the beginning of the Japanese American internment camps. Anyone with at least one-sixteenth Japanese blood was evacuated, including 17,000 children under the age of ten and the elderly and disabled. Altogether, 117,000 people were sent to internment camps.

12

MEDAL OF HONOR

There were thirteen Medal of Honor recipients from Michigan. Most of them were born and raised here, though some made their home here only after the war.

Ensign Francis C. Flaherty was in a gun turret on board the USS *Oklahoma* on December 7, 1941, when the ship was hit by three torpedoes. As the ship began to capsize, he remained in the turret, shining a light on the exit so that his fellow crewmen could escape. Flaherty was trapped in the turret with several other crewmen, and the ship completely rolled over before he could get out. Over the next few days, 32 men were rescued, but Flaherty was not one of them. A total of 429 men were trapped in the ship and were never rescued. Their remains were placed at the National Memorial Cemetery of the Pacific located in Honolulu. All of the graves are tombstones inscribed "Unknown," including Flaherty, but in a cemetery in his hometown of Charlotte, there is a memorial at the Maple Hill Cemetery.

Owen Francis Patrick Hammerberg was born in Daggett, Michigan, in the Upper Peninsula. He lived with his father in Flint and enlisted in the navy in July 1941. He served on battleship USS *Idaho* and sub chaser USS *Advent* before attending diving school. He trained to become a diver in 1944 and was assigned to the Pacific Fleet Salvage Force as boatswain second class at Pearl Harbor.

On February 17, 1945, Owen rescued two fellow divers trapped under a sunken troop ship in Pearl Harbor. He worked for several hours in black water forty feet deep and shifting mud. After freeing the first man, he continued to

Left: Ensign Francis C. Flaherty. *Right*: Owen Francis Patrick Hammerberg. *Photos courtesy of the Medal of Honor Museum, Patriots Point, South Carolina.*

work on freeing the second. A piece of heavy steel fell on him and pinned him over his friend. He kept the weight off his friend so that he could escape.

Owen later died in the hospital from the injuries he sustained. He was awarded the Medal of Honor. His parents, Jonas Hammerberg and Elizabeth Moss, accepted on his behalf. The official citation of his heroics reads, "For conspicuous gallantry and intrepidity at the risk of his life above and beyond the call of duty as a diver engaged in rescue operations at West Loch, Pearl Harbor." A destroyer escort was named in his honor in 1954 and christened by his mother. Two memorials honor Owen, a playground in Detroit at West Chicago and Wyoming and a monument at Veteran's Park in Stephenson by a VFW post.

Lieutenant Colonel Matt Urban, originally from Buffalo, New York, made his home in Michigan in 1949. His birth name was Matt Louis Urbanowicz. His father was a Polish immigrant and his mother was from Depew, New York. He was born in 1919 and attended East High School in Buffalo. He had three brothers, and one passed away in 1927. Matt attended Cornell University in Ithaca, New York, and graduated with a bachelor of arts degree in 1941.

Matt joined the military in 1941 and was commissioned second lieutenant of the infantry. By the time the war began, he had been promoted to first lieutenant and participated in the first landing in North Africa. He was wounded that first day, along with another soldier. This was his first of several Purple Heart medals. In Tunisia, a sergeant wrote that Matt was wounded and refused evacuation. He had taken out an enemy combat patrol single handedly, and as the unit was falling back, he grabbed a German soldier and killed him with a trench knife. Taking the dead German's machine pistol, he held back the advancing Germans, until he was injured with a grenade.

Lieutenant Colonel Matt Urban. *Photo courtesy of the Holland Historical Museum.*

Urban was evacuated and hospitalized. He returned to the fight in the invasion of Sicily. While he was on board the USS *Orizeba*, the ship was attacked by a German fighter. One of the ship's gunnery crew spotters was wounded. Urban immediately took over with the spotter's broken binoculars and sighted the fighter coming back. The gunnery crew was able to take out the German plane.

After the invasion of Sicily, the Germans were entrenched in a fortified mountain stronghold, and the First Infantry was bogged down. The Sixtieth Infantry, of which Urban was a part, was tasked with flanking the Germans by crossing the mountains with pack mules and four thousand men. They caught the Germans by surprise, and they retreated to Randazzo. Soon after, Urban was sent to England to rest and reequip to prepare for the invasion of Normandy, France.

Urban did not take part in the invasion on June 6, 1944, but did land at Utah Beach on June 11, 1944. F Company was hit by heavy German small arms, and a bazooka gunner was wounded. Urban picked up the bazooka and told the gunner's ammo carrier to follow. Making their way through the first hedgerow, Urban took out to German Panzer tanks. Later that day, he was wounded from shrapnel by a German tank. He refused to be evacuated and continued to give orders while sitting up and being carried on a stretcher. The next day, he was wounded again in the forearm and evacuated to a field hospital, where doctors operated on his left calf under lanterns at night. He was sent back to England for more treatment on a troop ship.

Not completely healed, Urban returned to Normandy in July 1944, when he learned that the army was lacking experienced officers. Limping and using a stick as a cane, he caught up with the second company of the Sixtieth Infantry. The men were bogged down by German defenses, and he was able to get them moving again. He also rescued a Sherman tank driver pinned in his burning tank before it exploded. A second tank that was in the area that was under siege lost its gunner and turret man, and the turret was not operable. A tank platoon leader informed Urban that because of a crossfire, they were unable to get anyone to handle the 50-caliber machine gun on the turret. Urban crawled along the side of the tank, climbed to the top to man the gun and ordered the driver to quickly move out of there. He fired on the gun emplacement, and the anti-tank gun was unable to hit the turret of the tank.

Immediately, the battalion rallied and attacked the Germans. Urban destroyed more machine gun positions and overran enemy lines. Much of this was hand-to-hand and bayonet fighting. All this was witnessed by the Second Battalion commander.

In August 1944, Urban was wounded in the chest, narrowly missing his heart, and again refused treatment. The battalion commander was killed on the August 6 near Cherbourg, France. Urban took command of the battalion and was wounded again and remained with the battalion. In September 1944, Urban was wounded again, but this time, the wound was more critical. He was wounded in the neck from two grenades that went off. It went through his larynx, permanently disabling it. He was treated and dragged to a ditch where a doctor provided more medical treatment, and a chaplain gave him his last rites. Amazingly, he survived, spending a few weeks in a French field hospital before being sent back to England for more rest. He was promoted to major. He returned to his battalion, hoping to take command again but was denied because of health issues and not being able to speak.

The army medically retired Urban in February 1946, giving him the rank of lieutenant colonel. He returned to the States and moved to Michigan and become recreation director in Port Huron. Later, he became director of Monroe Community Center. He made a final trip to Holland and continued to serve the community as a coach in basketball, baseball and boxing. He was also one of three trainers for Muhammad Ali for the San Francisco Olympics tryouts.

Urban took part in the community as a cubmaster for the Cub Scouts, was a member of the Red Cross and was inducted to the Hall of Honor for the Softball Hall of Fame. President Jimmy Carter presented him with the Medal of Honor in July 19, 1980. The day before, he was presented the Legion of Merit, Bronze Star Medal with "V" device (second oak leaf cluster) by the army chief of staff, Edward C. Meyer. That same day, at the French Embassy, Urban was presented the Croix de Guerre with Bronze Star by François Lefebvre de Laboulaye, the French ambassador. This citation was originally signed by General Charles de Gaulle in June 1944 but was not presented to him at the time.

Urban passed away in 1995 from a collapsed lung believed to be caused by his war injuries so many years before. He was laid to rest at Arlington National Cemetery.

Dirk J. Vlug joined the army and served in the Pacific theater. Dirk earned his Medal of Honor when he went beyond the call of duty near Limon, Leyte, Philippine Islands. The Americans hit a roadblock when they were attacked by Japanese tanks. Dirk left his covered position with a rocket launcher and six rounds of ammunition. He engaged heavy 37mm gun and machine gun fire and took on five enemy tanks.

The first tank was taken out with a single shot from the rocket launcher. The crew started to climb out of the second tank, but Dirk killed one of the

Urban receiving the Medal of Honor from President Jimmy Carter. *Photo courtesy of the Holland Historical Museum.*

members, forcing the other two to retreat inside for safety. Firing another rocket, he took out another tank. Soon after, three more tanks approached. He flanked the first one and destroyed it. Despite the enemy fire, he destroyed another. He used his last rocket to take out the last tank, which crashed down a steep embankment. With his bravery, he single-handedly accomplished the battalion's mission.

Dirk returned home to Grand Rapids to a hero's welcome.

Raymond Zussman from Hamtramck joined the army in September 1941 and rose to the rank of second lieutenant. Zussman earned the Medal of Honor on September 12, 1944, when he and the two tank crews and infantry under his command were bogged down by enemy fire near Noroy le Bourg, France, occupied by the German army. After losing one tank to enemy fire, Zussman took it upon himself to locate the enemy on foot, returning only to instruct the remaining tank crew where to direct fire on the enemy.

As Zussman continued on foot, he and his men encountered a roadblock just fifty yards in front of them. He instructed the crew to fire on the roadblock, and as he was exposed to enemy fire, three Germans were killed and eight more were captured. As the crew advanced on a group of houses that the enemy occupied with a machine gun and small arms, the Germans fired on Zussman, which kicked up dust in front of him. He ordered the tank crew he guided to fire on the enemy. Twenty more Germans surrendered, and Zussman and his unit continued to advance, encountering more Germans in another house. The Germans threw a few grenades and fired at Zussman, and another fifteen Germans surrendered. Zussman had decided to go around a house out of sight of his men, and his men could hear Zussman firing his rifle. He returned with thirty more German prisoners. Altogether, eighteen Germans were killed, and ninety-two were taken prisoner.

Nine days later, in a different battle, Zussman was killed. He was posthumously awarded the Medal of Honor. The people of Hamtramck named a small park in front of St. Francis Hospital after him. In later years, the hospital closed, but the city converted the building to become city hall, and the park remains as Zussman Park.

John Sjogren from Rockford, Michigan, was serving with the army in the Pacific theater, with the rank of sergeant. He was a squad leader and was ordered to take out a Japanese position on the top of a hill. This was near San Jose Hacienda in the Philippines. The enemy was well entrenched with automatic weapons in what were called spider holes and two hidden pillboxes, making it difficult to advance.

Left: Dirk J. Vlug. *Photos courtesy of the Grand Rapids Public Library.*

Raymond Zussman. *Photo courtesy of the Hamtramck Historical Society.*

After realizing that his buddy was killed, Sjogren started tossing grenades into the spider holes, which were dug out by the Japanese to hide from unsuspecting Americans. These holes were located around pillboxes with Japanese machine guns.

After returning from war, Sjorgern was presented with the Medal of Honor, and the community of Rockford presented him with the first postwar Ford, built in 1946.

Sergeant Oscar Johnson from Foster City protected his company's left flank on his own to break through the German line with a seven-man squad. His squad was at a standstill when it encountered heavy resistance from the Germans. A mortar gunner spent all his ammo and turned to using a rifle. All of Johnson's men were wounded or killed by that afternoon on September 16, 1944. The enemy was so close to his position that he was able to throw a few hand grenades. At one point, he stood up and fired his rifle at the enemy, and twenty-five Germans surrendered to Johnson.

Two men were sent to give assistance but ended up taking cover from heavy mortar fire and were wounded. With no regard to his own safety, Johnson rushed to the hole where the men were half-buried. A medical corpsman was able to make it to Johnson's position and provide medical assistance to the wounded. Johnson covered their position by firing back at the enemy while the men were evacuated to safety. Five companies of German paratroopers attacked Johnson's company without success. Twenty Germans were found around Johnson's position.

Born in West Virginia, Private First Class Walter G. Wetzel joined the army in Roseville in July 1941. Wetzel paid the ultimate price to receive his Medal of Honor. On April 3, 1945, Wetzel threw himself on top of a German grenade to smother the blast. Wetzel was posthumously awarded the Medal of Honor six months later, on February 26, 1946, by President Harry Truman.

Coming back from his first mission, waist gunner Sergeant Maynard H. Smith's plane was shot several times by fighters and antiaircraft artillery.

Left: A statue was erected of John Sjogren in front of the town's historical museum. *Photos courtesy of the Rockford Historical Museum.*

The oxygen supply was cut off, and two of the men were wounded. The plane was on fire, and the radio room was shot up. With no communication with the pilot and copilot, Smith remained at his post defending with the workable guns. While still fighting off German fighters, Smith used up all of the fire extinguishers to try to put out the fire. Three of the men had bailed out over the ocean while Smith was putting out the fire. The fire had ignited ammunition and melted the camera in the radio room along with a gun turret. Smith was able to finish putting out the fire by wrapping himself up with clothing. He was able to give first aid to the tail gunner while putting out the fire and defending the plane from the enemy. His gallantry and loyalty to his plane and fellow crew members, with no regard for his own life, was an inspiration for the U.S. Armed Forces and was deserving of the Medal of Honor.

Demas T. Craw was born in Long Lake Township with his twin brother Theron and attended school in Traverse City. He dropped out of high school to join the army during World War I. He was discharged at the rank of private first class and sent to officers' training school in Georgia. He was discharged in 1919, only to join the army in Grand Rapids to pursue the career as an officer.

Above, left: Sergeant Oscar Johnson. *Photo courtesy of the National Museum of the United States Air Force.*

Above, right: Private First Class Walter G. Wetzel. *Photo courtesy of the Medal of Honor Museum, Patriots Point, South Carolina.*

Left: Lieutenant Colonel Demas T. Craw. *Photo courtesy of the National Museum of the United States Air Force.*

Craw attended West Point and had his sights set on becoming a pilot for the Army Air Corps. That almost ended when he suffered an eye injury while playing polo. After his eye healed, he applied for pilot training.

He served in many different pursuit squadrons before World War II and became an observer in China, Romania, Egypt, Libya, the Dutch East Indies (now Indonesia) and India. His observance of the air commands of different countries' air forces gave him the knowledge of bomber tactics.

Demas didn't earn his medal as a pilot, though. In November 1941, he was promoted to lieutenant colonel. He sailed with an invasion force from the state of Virginia to North Africa. Demas volunteered to help another Army Air Forces officer, Major Pierpont M. Hamilton, an intelligence officer. They were tasked with delivering a message to the French in Morocco. The message would set up a cease-fire with the French.

Under heavy fire, they were unable to land at the designated area because of shell fire. They managed to get ashore and find a truck to make their way to the French headquarters. Friendly fire from their own ships made it difficult to make their way through the town. Nearing Port Lyautey, Craw was killed instantly by machine gun fire from a concealed enemy position near the road.

Francis Junior Pierce was a pharmacist's mate first class in the U.S. Navy. He earned his Medal of Honor at Iwo Jima, on March 15 and 16, 1945. Francis was attached to the Second Battalion, Twenty-Fourth Marines, Fourth Marine Division and volunteered for the most dangerous assignments. While carrying men to a forward aid station, the group encountered heavy machine gun fire. Pierce took charge when one corpsman and two of the eight stretcher carriers were wounded. He carried the newly wounded men to shelter and gave first aid. He directed the evacuation of three of the casualties and stood in the open to draw fire from the enemy while he fired back at them. This allowed the carriers to reach cover. He then continued to administer first aid to one of the two men and stopped his bleeding. A Japanese soldier fired from a cave and wounded Pierce's patient. Pierce risked his own live to save his patient and deliberately exposed himself to the enemy to draw him out of his cave. He used the last of his ammunition to take him out. He then carried the wounded man on his back, unarmed and exposed, in open terrain. Exhausted, Pierce went back and rescued the remaining marines.

The following morning, he was seriously wounded by a sniper while giving aid to a wounded marine. Despite his injuries, he refused medical treatment and provided protective fire for his comrades to do their job. He returned home to become a police officer for the city of Grand Rapids.

Jesse R. Drowley was born in St. Charles on September 9, 1919. His act of gallantry was in the Pacific Theater on Bougainville in the Solomon Islands. While searching for the enemy, he and his men stumbled on a bunker and came under machine gun fire. With three of his men badly wounded, he rushed to rescue two of them. He noticed the tanks that were in the area

Left: Pharmacist's Mate First Class Francis Junior Pierce. *Photo courtesy of the Grand Rapids Public Library.*

Right: Jesse R. Drowley. *Photo courtesy of the Medal of Honor Museum on board the USS* Yorktown *in Mount Pleasant, South Carolina.*

could not see the bunker that was firing up them. He had another soldier help rescue the third man and ran across open terrain to one of the tanks. He signaled to the tank crew that he would guide them to the bunker and rode on top of the tank and exchanged his weapon for a submachine gun. The tank was under constant fire and got within twenty feet of the pillbox where the enemy was. Drowley received a severe bullet wound to the chest. He refused medical treatment and continued to stay on top of the tank until the tank crew could take out the pillbox. He was wounded again and lost his left eye and fell to the ground. He remained with the tank until the pillbox was destroyed. Drowley returned on his own to receive medical attention.

Major Charles Thomas, born in Birmingham, Alabama, moved to Detroit when he was a child. He joined the army in 1942 and trained as an infantryman but later joined a newly formed tank destroyer unit. Thomas achieved the rank of second lieutenant and was attached to the 614th Tank Destroyer Unit, a Black unit. He knew that there would be problems, since the equipment was outdated and breaking down compared to the equipment that the White units had. Just like Coleman Young, he realized that there would be discrimination when the Black officers were not allowed to use the officers' club and there were no recreational facilities for the Black personnel.

The men grew tired of endless training and were eager to fight. They got their chance to fight, and Thomas's morale was inspired when his unit was attached to the Third Army under the command of General George Patton. Patton did not care if the unit was Black or White. All that mattered was that they could fight. Politics still played a key factor, though, and the unit had outdated equipment that would constantly break down.

Thomas earned the Distinguished Service Cross for his heroism in the capture of an occupied German town of Climbach five miles from the French-German border. The only road into the town was up a hill. As a

Major Charles Thomas. *Photo courtesy of the Medal of Honor Museum, Patriots Point, South Carolina.*

diversion, Thomas took the lead in a scout car and went straight up the hill while the infantry snuck through the woods into town. On the foggy morning of December 14, 1944, as Thomas advanced, the Germans opened with artillery and tank fire. At first, the windshield was blown out and shattered and then the tires were blown out. Though he was wounded over most of his body, Thomas still took charge and fired back on the German forces. They held off the Germans for over five hours, wearing them down, until the advancing infantry that snuck through the woods finally took the town. His unit became the first to receive the first distinguished citation, and he was promoted to captain. In the unit were eight Silver Stars, twenty-eight Bronze Stars and seventy-nine Purple Hearts.

Thomas's unit advanced through Austria and Germany, but he did not. He sat out the rest of the war in the Percy Jones Veterans Hospital in Battle Creek. He was discharged in 1947, with the rank of major. Because of his wounds, he received disability benefits for the rest of his life, and while his son was growing up, some of the veterans he ran into thought he was killed back at Climbach. After his passing in 1980, and because of stories of his valor, he was awarded the Medal of Honor posthumously.

13

OUR HOMETOWN HEROES

Many people are unaware of the local heroes who served during the war. One of these heroes would become president of the United States during a time of mistrust in the government. Another would make his fame as a weatherman for television and radio. Some would come to Michigan for training, and another hero from another state would make Michigan his home after a baseball team traded him for a catcher.

Born and raised in the Detroit area, Marvin Eliot Schlossberg (Sonny Eliot) learned to fly at Wayne County Airport in 1939. When World War II began, Sonny signed up for the Army Air Corps on December 8, 1941, the day after Pearl Harbor was attacked. Already an accomplished pilot, he was given the rank of second lieutenant and trained to fly the most produced bomber in the United States, the B-24 Liberator. He felt comfortable and safe flying this aircraft after a stunt his instructor had performed with the plane. Sonny said, "He had done the most amazing thing. He made sure everyone was strapped in and at a high enough altitude. The instructor took the plane into a barrel roll, proving the plane was safe to fly."

Sonny enjoyed flying the B-24, but in joking, he said he owed the United States two planes. The first one he lost flying over the mountains out West. One of the engines caught fire, and he could not get enough altitude to clear the mountains. He and the crew had to bail out, and the plane crashed. After the war, the U.S. government sent him a bill for that plane. He and the crew all agreed that it had to have been sabotaged. The second time, he was over Germany, and he could not be held accountable. The Germans shot him down.

Photos courtesy of Sonny Elliot.

Sonny was assigned to the 577th Bomber Group in the 8th Army Air Forces. Its base was in Norwich, England. He flew a B-24J that was built at the Willow Run Plant. His last mission was to bomb a factory in Goethe, Germany, that produced ball bearings for the Messerschmitt ME109 fighters. He and his crew dropped their bombs on the factory and started for home, when a German fighter headed straight toward them and shot them down. One of the waist gunners was injured, but the high altitude slowed the bleeding. They all bailed out of the plane. The crew attached a parachute to the injured man and pulled the ripcord as they pushed him out of the plane.

Sonny was the last man to bail out. He landed in a snow-covered field and lost his boots when he bailed out. Noticing a barn, he tried to hide. The door was locked, and a civilian pointing a rifle at him captured him and turned him in to the local authorities. Eventually, the Germans picked him up and questioned him. He was questioned about the radar that many of the planes were equipped with, and he said he knew nothing about it. They also asked about his religion, and though he was Jewish, he told them that he was Lutheran, because he had lost his dog tags after bailing out of the plane.

Sonny and his copilot were finally sent to Stalag 1, a POW camp. There, they met up with their bombardier. At the camp, the Jewish Americans were separated from the other denominations and were to be transported to a different camp, but this did not happen. The Jewish Americans did share one building in the camp and were still able to converse with the other prisoners. Sonny felt guilty about not being with his fellow Jewish people, so he consulted with the chaplain who was in the camp. The chaplain ordered him to keep his mouth shut. Every day while imprisoned there, he lived in fear that the Germans would learn his secret and that he and the other Jews would be removed and sent to another camp.

The photo taken by the Germans after Sonny was captured. *Photo courtesy of Sonny Elliot.*

The Red Cross was a blessing to the soldiers at the camp. It provided blankets, food and even books with blank pages. The men kept journals of their stay in the camp, and many of them were artistic. If someone drew something interesting, many of them would request the same drawing for their journal. Sonny kept his journal, and at the end, he had a leather book cover made of a boxing glove and a set of pilot wings embedded in the cover with the letter *k* in the center. The *k* stood for *Kriegsgafangenen*, German for "prisoner of war." The guards just called them *Kreigs* for short.

The Germans did their best to discourage the prisoners, but unknown to the Germans, the prisoners had a radio to listen to the British broadcasting news of the war. Sonny became the morale officer and put on elaborate shows with the men who had talent. He even choreographed many of the shows and printed programs and tickets. On the programs, he used the name Sonny Eliot, which would be the name he later used when broadcasting the weather report.

The camp across the road was a concentration camp for Russian POWs. Sonny found out that the Russians were being executed like the Jews. When he talked about this in an oral interview for the Holocaust Center in Bloomfield Hills, Michigan, he found it very difficult to speak about.

When Sonny was liberated from the camp, he spent time in Paris before returning to the United States. Sonny's crew survived the war, including the injured waist gunner. He found out about this later when he and some of the men went to the commandant's office to see what was on file.

Sonny suspected that the Germans thought he was Jewish after finding his file and on a card was marked "Juda" meaning Jewish. He kept many of these items in his journal.

Gerald Rudolph Ford, our thirty-eighth president, served in the U.S. Navy during World War II. He was born in Omaha, Nebraska, as Leslie Lynch King Jr. His mother left his father because of spousal abuse and moved back to her parents in Illinois. Ford later changed his name to Gerald R. Ford Jr., after his stepfather. Just before the war, he had completed the bar exam to practice law and opened a law firm with a friend. Then the Japanese attacked Pearl Harbor, and he enlisted in the navy. He started off with the rank of ensign in the naval reserve and later became a full-time officer and taught naval skills in Annapolis, Maryland. He was promoted a couple of times and became a lieutenant by 1943. He applied for active ship duty and was assigned to the USS *Monterey* as assistant navigator, athletic officer and antiaircraft battery officer. He and the ship served in several actions in the Pacific theater with the Third and Fifth Fleets. His ship did not receive any damage from the Japanese but did receive damage from a typhoon that hit Admiral Halsey's third fleet. Several destroyers were lost, along with eight hundred men. Ford almost became a causality when he was on the bridge and the ship started to roll twenty-five degrees.

The camp band that Sonny organized to entertain his fellow POWs. *Photo courtesy of Sonny Elliot.*

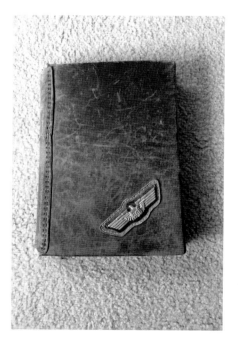

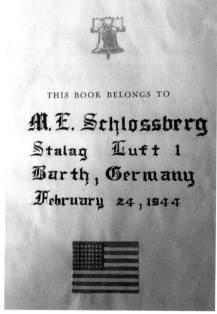

Left: Sonny's personal journal from the POW camp. *Right*: Excerpt from Sonny's journal. *Photos courtesy of Sonny Elliot.*

Above: Marvin E. Schlossberg, better known as Sonny Elliot. *Photo courtesy of Sonny Elliott.*

Right: A young Lieutenant Gerald R. Ford holding a sexton for navigation. *Photos courtesy of the Frankenmuth Historical Museum.*

USS *Monterey. Photo courtesy of the Gerald R. Ford Presidential Library.*

He fell over the side and caught the railing and climbed back aboard. On the USS *Monterey*, a fire broke out below deck because of some aircraft sliding around from the typhoon. Halsey ordered Captain Ingersoll to abandon ship. Ingersoll ignored that order and ordered Ford to go below deck and deal with the fire.

Ford was reassigned to Pre-Flight School at St. Mary's College of California, where he coached football until January 1946 and achieved the rank of lieutenant commander. He was eventually sent to the Navy's Separation Center to be processed out under honorable conditions on February 23, 1946. By June 1946, the secretary of the navy accepted Ford's resignation from the naval reserve.

Born and raised in the Detroit area, Eddie Slovik was the only soldier executed for desertion during the war. No one had been executed for desertion since the Civil War. Eddie had a troublesome life growing up. He was arrested at the age of twelve for stealing food. Because he had a criminal record when the United States declared war, he was ineligible to join the armed forces. He was classified as 4-F. It wasn't until he married Antoinette Wisniewski in 1942 and gained employment that he became eligible to join.

When he was deployed in Europe, Eddie finally saw combat. Taking cover from artillery shelling, Eddie came to the realization that he could get killed. Eddie became separated from his unit and was picked up by a Canadian unit and spent several months with them as a cook. Eventually, he was returned to the U.S. Army and his unit. Eddie felt that he couldn't go back to the frontlines and asked for a transfer. The transfer was rejected, and he refused to go to the frontlines and fight.

His refusal meant court-martial. His punishment was execution by firing squad. Eddie wrote a letter to General Eisenhower, pleading to give him leniency and allow him to go back to the frontlines and fight. Eisenhower said that he couldn't find it in his heart to allow this and that he would leave his friends in battle again to die.

Eddie was executed by firing squad and placed in an unmarked grave in France. Over the years, Eddie's widow tried to have his body returned to Michigan to be buried and to get his pension. Others petitioned seven presidents, from Harry Truman to Jimmy Carter, for a pardon. After Antoinette's death in 1979, Macomb County commissioner Bernard V. Calka took up the cause in 1981. It wasn't until 1987 that Calka persuaded then president Ronald Reagan to allow Eddie's remains transferred to Woodmere Cemetery and reburied next to his wife.

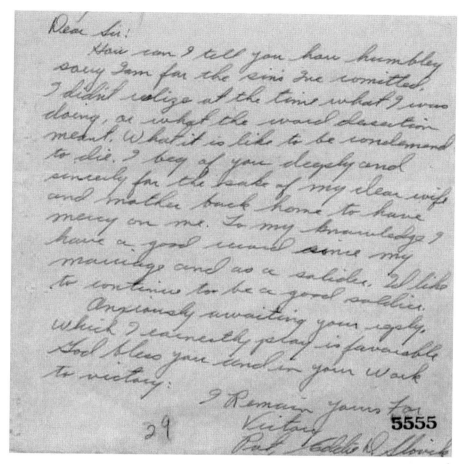

Excerpt of Eddie Slovik's letter to General Eisenhower. *Letter courtesy of the Franklin D. Roosevelt Library.*

Nancy Harkness was born in the Upper Peninsula in Houghton in 1914. She was the daughter of a doctor, and when she was a young girl, a pair of barnstormers flew into town. They were charging a penny per pound for anyone who wanted a ride in their airplanes. Nancy convinced her parents to let her save up to get flying lessons. She was able to get her pilot's license at the age of sixteen, just before going off to college. She attended Vassar College for a short time, until her father could no longer afford to pay for her education. Through a friend who took her on as an instructor, she met her husband, Robert Love. They married, and both continued flying airmail.

Nancy was soon introduced to Joan Cochran, a fellow pilot, and the two became friends. When war broke out in Europe, Joan recruited twenty-

Above: Nancy in the pilot seat of a B-17 Flying Fortress. *Photo courtesy of Texas Woman University.*

Right: A young Paul Fried. *Photo courtesy of Hope College.*

Photo courtesy of Hope College.

five female pilots to ferry planes in England. Soon after, the United States entered the war and decided to work with Nancy, who was forming the Women Auxiliary Ferrying Squadron (WAFS), and General "Hap" Arnold to form the Women Airforce Service Squadron. These three convinced the U.S. government to allow experienced women pilots to fly planes for the military to allow men to go off to combat. The government formed the WAFS first to operate with the Army Air Transport Command.

The women who flew for Air Transport Command paved the way for the WASP to be formed. These women towed targets, tested planes and flew cargo and personnel around the continental United States. Nancy learned to fly many aircraft, including the B-17 Flying Fortress. She tried to fly a B-17 to England, until General "Hap" Arnold got word of this and stopped her in Newfoundland, Canada. General Arnold believed that women should not be flying in combat areas, and if a woman were to be injured or killed, it would be bad public relations for the military.

While General Turner, commander of Air Transport Command, was with Nancy in a B-17, she experienced a problem with one of the engines. They landed at the Traverse City Naval Base, and a young ensign came up to the plane and ordered her to fly back out. She explained that they had an engine problem. General Turner tried to find out what the problem was and even showed his stars from the cockpit of the plane. The ensign still insisted that they had to leave. Turner asked Nancy if they could take off and if there were any other fields they could go to. Nancy said they could still fly to Cadillac. Nancy stuck her head out the window and said to the ensign, "Unless you want a face full of prop then you need to get out of the way."

Toward the end of 1944, the WAFS and WASP were disbanded after an attempt to get full military status. Nancy was so upset that she burned her uniforms and anything pertaining to the military after the war was over. Nancy received the Air Medal for her leadership in training and assigning three hundred women in advanced military aircraft. In 1948, she became a lieutenant colonel in the United States Air Force Reserves. She had three daughters and passed away in 1976 of cancer.

In Holland, Michigan, two refugees from Austria who escaped Europe in 1939 were attending Hope College. When war broke out, refugees from countries that the United States was at war with had to prove their patriotism. Holland High School offered a citizenship course called Class in Americanism. These people had two months to reregister their citizenship. Paul Fried, one of the refugees, had enlisted in the army and was assigned to work in intelligence. When the war ended in Germany, he was a translator

Boogie Woogie Bugler Calms 6AM Beefs, Swings First Call

Pfc Clarence Zylman's version of First Call draws the last thing anyone would expect from a 6 AM audience—applause.

The men in Zylman's company aren't crazy either, they just appreciate the hot licks he puts into his rendition of the traditional soldier's eye-opener.

It happened this way: Back before he came into the Army, Zylman, of Muskegon, Mich., was a trumpeter in Tommy Tucker's dance orchestra. Instead of winding up as a cook or a medic—as old soldiers know he should have done—Zylman was made bugler.

He wasn't used to being yelled at when he was doing his stuff, and he soon decided that it was the tune that was wrong, not the way he played it. Any solid sender worth his stuff knows how to improvise, and Zylman figured that First Call needed a little rewriting.

He doped out a swing version that rolled sleepy soldiers out smiling and had 'em climbing into their clothes with speed, willingness and a hot cha cha.

Now the boogie-woogie bugler is on tour with a Special Service Unit.

This article was found by Kurt Trautman in an issue of *Stars and Stripes* from Saturday, March 20, 1943.

during the Nuremberg Trials. After the trials, Fried finished his studies at Hope College, where he joined the history department.

The Andrews sisters made "The Boogie Woogie Bugle Boy of Company B" a popular song among GIs and civilians. These ladies even performed this song in a movie with Abbott and Costello called *Buck Privates*. It's not known whether the songwriter, Don Raye, who collaborated with Hughie Prince, composed the song about a particular soldier, but the U.S. Army stated that the trumpeter soldier was from Muskegon, Michigan.

Clarence Zylman from Muskegon was not the athletic type in school but found playing the cornet in the band much more satisfying. He dropped out of high school at the age of seventeen and made his way to Chicago to play with the big bands, like Paul Specht and Tommy Tucker Orchestra. Learning the style of the times in music, he helped lead the nation in the boogie woogie music revolution.

After the attack on Pearl Harbor, Clarence joined the U.S. Army at the age of thirty-five. He was not assigned to the army band right away. He worked with the Army Corps of Engineers building airfields in Europe, and while he had his skills as a trumpet player, he would play "Reveille," "Taps" and many other military tunes as a bugler. As a professional musician, he had spiced up reveille one morning and caught the attention of the commanding general. When called to the general's office, he thought he was going to be reprimanded. Instead, the officer praised his style and told him that he liked

Statue of Clarence Zylman located at the LST-393 Veterans Museum. *Photo courtesy of Kurt Trautman.*

the fact that the men had a little more spring in their step. Clarence was assigned to the army band, and he taught others to play the bugle. Although the song came out before Clarence joined the service, the army made it clear to newspapers who the Boogie Woogie Bugle Boy was. *Stars and Stripes* also made it clear that it was Clarence. When the war ended, Clarence returned home as a decorated soldier. He did something he had not thought about before the war: getting married. He also found it difficult to get steady work as a musician, for the big band era was coming to an end, with singers like Frank Sinatra coming on the scene. His wife passed away in 1959, and with a broken heart, he never played again. Clarence did remarry and went to work in the automotive industry. He posed in his uniform and trumpet many years later.

Charles H. Lindbergh was the first man to fly across the Atlantic Ocean, from New York to Paris, and he started Trans World Airlines. Lindbergh's mother was a schoolteacher in the Detroit area, and he became good friends with Henry Ford. Lindbergh was a colonel with the army reserve and tried to obtain active duty status when the United States entered the war. He was very outspoken before the war that the Germans had superior air power, and this did not sit well with the military and government. For that, he made a few political enemies.

Charles Lindberg visiting Selfridge after his flight from New York to Paris. *Photo courtesy of the Selfridge Military Air Museum.*

Left: Governor William G. Milliken. *Photo courtesy of the Traverse City Library*. *Right*: U.S. House of Representative member John Dingell Jr. *Personal collection.*

Lindberg wanted to fight, but the army and politicians were afraid to lose an American hero. He worked at the Willow Run Bomber Plant and with other aircraft manufacturers as a consultant because of his friendship with Ford, who allowed him to test-fly B-24 bombers and use his knowledge as a pilot.

The forty-fourth governor of Michigan served during World War II. William Milliken was attending Yale University before the war broke out. It wasn't until after his junior year that he enlisted in the Army Air Corps. William met the love of his life while training to be a gunner on a B-24 Liberator bomber. He met Helen Wallbank at a dance in Topeka. They dated while he was training, and before being deployed, he asked her to marry him after the war. They corresponded with each other while he was overseas.

In a biography about Milliken, *William G. Milliken Michigan's Passionate Moderate*, he told the story of one memorable mission. His plane was badly damaged, and the pilot tried to fly back to their field. Thirty miles out, the plane's hydraulics went out, and they were only able to lower one side of the landing gear. The pilot made the call to bail out of the plane. With the plane on autopilot, the pilot and copilot bailed. William noticed this before he bailed out of the plane. The plane appeared to be heading out to sea but unfortunately lost control and eventually crashed on land, killing a farmer in his field.

William survived two crash landings and received seven military honors, including a Purple Heart and the Air Medal. After being honorably

"Jumpin" Joe Beyrle POW photo.
Photo courtesy of the USS Silversides Submarine Museum.

discharged in October 1945, he married Helen Wallbank.

William was involved in politics after the war, and from January 22, 1969, to January 1, 1983, he was Michigan's governor. Milliken passed away on October 16, 2019.

John Dingell Jr. was the longest-serving representative in the U.S. Congress, serving for fifty-nine years. Before he joined the military, Dingell attended Georgetown Preparatory School and then House Page School. He served as a page for the House of Representatives until he turned eighteen in 1944 and then enlisted in the army. John was present when President Franklin D. Roosevelt gave his famous speech to Congress that the Japanese attacked Pearl Harbor. John had risen to the rank of second lieutenant, and in November 1945, he was given orders to participate in the invasion of Japan. It was said that President Truman giving the order to drop the atomic bomb on Hiroshima saved his life.

"Jumpin" Joe Beyrle had a scholarship to Harvard University when the war broke out. He turned it down to join the army. Joe trained with the 101st Airborne Division, and on D-Day, June 6, 1941, he got separated from his unit. Joe found French freedom fighters and fought with them until he was captured by the Germans and became a POW. This did not stop Joe one bit, as he escaped and tried to make his way to the western front to rejoin the fighting. Unfortunately, he was captured again. He was tortured by the Gestapo and constantly interrogated as a spy. He was released to the German army to be placed in another POW camp. Joe escaped again and was captured again. The third time Joe escaped, instead of heading to the western front, he headed east and came across a Russian tank unit commanded by a woman by the name of Aleksandra Samusenko. Joe convinced her to allow him to help in the fighting with his knowledge of explosives.

While Joe was captured, his dog tags were with another fallen American soldier. This led the U.S. Army to assume that he was dead, so a letter was sent to his family, stating that he died in action. Services were held in church. His parents found out at the end of the war that he survived.

Left: Ernie Harwell. *Photo courtesy of the Detroit Public Library. Right: Personal collection.*

The Russian battalion that Joe fought with liberated his former POW camp Stalag II, where they found his photo taken by the Germans in the commandants' office. Soon after, he was injured by a German dive bomber. Joe was evacuated to a Soviet hospital in Poland. He received a visit from Soviet marshal Georgy Zhukov. As Joe was the only non-Soviet combatant in the hospital, Zhukov was intrigued by his story and provided him with official papers to rejoin the American forces.

Beyrle returned home and married Joanne Hollowell in 1946, at the very same church that had held his burial services. On June 6, 1996, the fiftieth anniversary of D-Day, Joe was honored by President Bill Clinton and Russian president Boris Yeltsin for his unique service. He is the only American to be decorated by the Russians for World War II.

Although not originally from Michigan, Ernie Harwell became synonymous with the state as the voice of Tigers baseball. Harwell joined the Tigers broadcast team in 1960 and, except for a brief spell in 1992, remained with the franchise until 2002. Before his career in baseball play-by-play, Harwell served in the U.S. Marines during World War II. As a war correspondent, he broadcast news for the home front. Toward the end of the war, Ernie visited Wake Island. In the beginning of the war, the American commander of Wake Island asked for reinforcements to defend the island. The island was surrounded by the Japanese, and the U.S. Navy was unable to supply armament, supplies and men. Eventually, the island was overrun by the Japanese and, who took control of the island. The marines who defended the island were sent to POW camps off the island. The civilian engineers who were building up defenses for the marines were forced into slave labor for the Japanese to rebuild the defenses with underground bunkers on the island, in case the Americans staged an attack on the island. The U.S. military would not retake the island but instead bypassed it. The Japanese were then cut off from receiving supplies. The Japanese commander became furious that the Americans bypassed the island. The Japanese commander executed the civilian engineers. When the Japanese military surrendered, the Japanese commander committed suicide. Ernie and other correspondents learned of the fate of the civilian engineers who were captured at the beginning of the war on Wake Island. After retiring from broadcasting in 2002, Ernie called an inning here and there until 2007. He died in Novi in 2010.

14

THE ARSENAL OF DEMOCRACY

I t was a well-known fact the automotive industry played a big part in the nation's production of weapons of war. The leaders of industry were called to Washington, D.C., to discuss what to do for the readiness of war materials. With our allies needing help, automotive companies had already begun the change to war production materials before the United States entered the war. Ford Motor Company had a government contract to build a factory that could assemble bombers, as well as jeeps, tanks and gliders. Chrysler and General Motors were contracted to build tanks, DUYKS, trucks, bombs and aircraft parts. One interesting fact is McCord Radiator Company made over twenty million steel helmets that the soldiers wore for protection. Other companies, like Packard, built engines for planes and PT boats. Studebaker built trucks and amphibious vehicles. Batham designed the jeep, but because it was not capable of mass producing the vehicle, the contract was awarded to Willy and Ford. Batham was chosen to build the utility trailer to accompany the jeep.

Henry Ford was the only American to help the Soviet Union build the automotive assembly line to build cars before World War II. Ford also admired Adolf Hitler and Nazism and had a plant to build Fords in Cologne, Germany. During the war and after his son Edsel passed away, Henry Ford, as much he did not want the United States to enter the war, resumed control of the company. Edsel died of liver cancer. With growing concerns about the loss of profit, the U.S. government considering taking over the company. Bill Knudsen, who was in charge of war production across the United States,

Illustration of the Borg Warner plant in Kalamazoo. *Courtesy of Borg Warner.*

had arranged for Edsel's son Henry Ford II to return home from the navy. Henry II returned to work in management. Toward the end of the war, Henry II took over the company, allowing Henry Sr. to resume retirement. He hired younger men after the war. They were involved with designing and building war machines. Ford Motor Company produced jeeps, tanks, support vehicles aircraft parts and the B-24 Liberator bomber. At one point, Henry met with General Hap Arnold at Wayne County Airport with a new truck for the army and went to the Willow Run Bomber Plant and signed one of the bombers.

It wasn't just women who were hired by Ford Motor Company to build B-24 bombers at Willow Run Bomber Plant. There were small places that people could not fit for riveting portions of the plane. Many plants hired little people for the job. At Willow Run, some of the people who were hired had previously worked as extras for the film *The Wizard of Oz.*

Even though there was employee housing at the Willow Run Bomber Plant, many employees had to commute to the plant from Detroit and other communities. Edsel Bryant Ford had to endure that commute as well. After

Right: Henry Ford with General Arnold in a Ford-built military truck. *Photo courtesy of the Detroit Metro Airport Historical Society.*

Below: *Photo courtesy of the Ypsilanti Historical Museum.*

Some of the workers at the Willow Run Bomber Plant. *Photos courtesy of the Ypsilanti Historical Museum.*

Photo courtesy of TACOM.

long discussions with the government, an expressway was constructed. At first, the expressway was called the Willow Run Highway, and Edsel died of cancer before it was completed. After the end of the war, the highway was extended east and was designated as Interstate 94. There was a ribbon-cutting ceremony and a naming of the highway in honor of Edsel Ford. Edsel's wife, Clara Jane Bryant Ford, cut the ribbon, along with his youngest son, William Clay Ford, and his wife, Martha Firestone Ford.

New and old tanks, trucks, cars and other equipment manufactured by the automotive industry went through a series of tests at the proving grounds belonging to the auto companies. They had to be sure there were no defects in the equipment, otherwise it could cost a soldier's life. Vigorous testing was done to everything produced by the automotive companies.

In many cases, if a defect was found in testing, the vehicle could be taken apart to find out the cause of the problem. It could be something as simple as a bolt or a crack in a part caused in the metal diecast. Many times, the defect or problem would be taken care of after the vehicle came off the assembly line.

Nash-Kelvinator had a contract to produce the R4 helicopter. There were three plants that built parts in Michigan for the helicopter and one that assembled them. Some of these helicopters were used in a classified project known as Ivory Soap. In the Pacific theater, the Japanese were a formidable

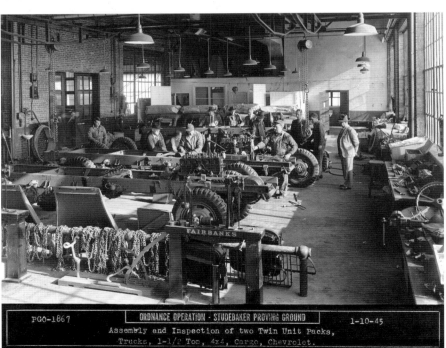

ORDNANCE OPERATION - STUDEBAKER PROVING GROUND

PGO-1867   1-10-45

Assembly and Inspection of two Twin Unit Packs,
Trucks, 1-1/2 Ton, 4x4, Cargo, Chevrolet.

Opposite: Photos courtesy of TACOM.

Above: Edsel Ford's wife, Clara, cuts the ribbon of the renamed Willow Run Highway to the Edsel Ford Expressway. Edsel's son William Clay Ford and daughter-in-law Martha Firestone Ford were by her side. *Photo courtesy of Ford Motor Company.*

Below: Helicopter landing on one of the army's aircraft repair ships. *Photo courtesy of the Library of Congress.*

foe in the air. The idea was that if a plane was badly damaged, it could be repaired by mechanics on board one of six Liberty ships or one of eighteen smaller support ships. These ships were equipped with cranes, machine guns to protect the ship from enemy planes and helicopter deck and machinery to make parts for the planes. If a plane had to make an emergency landing on the water, the pilot and crew would be rescued. If a plane was salvageable, it would be brought on one of the ships. As soon as the plane was repaired, it could be returned to service.

In the late 1980s, a movie called *Tucker* was created, depicting a man who wants to take on the big three automotive companies with his own car, the Tucker Torpedo, in 1948. Before the war, Tucker had many different jobs,

Preston Tucker and wife Vera. *Photo courtesy of the Ypsilanti Historical Museum.*

An artist sketch of the famous Tucker Torpedo. *Photo courtesy of the Ypsilanti Historical Museum.*

"Guam"
Aug. 16, 1945

My Dear Miss Zucharuck.

On behalf of myself and several of the fellows, we would like for you to know that you packed the last Photo Flash Bomb to fall on Japan. We found your address in the bomb crate, when we loaded it on the last B-29 to make a mission over Japan. We thought we would express our thanks to you. We would like for you to put this in your local newspaper to show our gratitude to you and the many others like you, that did so much to help win the war. I repeat, you packed the last Photo Flash Bomb to fall on Japan proper, from our B-29 base on this last mission of the war from this base. The boys would like a clipping from your newspaper if it should be printed, where we could

The letter to Olga Zucharuck from the airmen overseas. *Letter courtesy of the Rochester Historical Museum.*

including as a police officer in Lincoln Park, Michigan. He worked for a service station on the assembly line for Ford Motor Company and sold cars for many different dealerships. Just before the war, he started an aircraft company known as Tucker Aviation Company, operated out of his machine tool and die shop next to his home in Ypsilanti. He had plans to build a fighter for the Army Air Corps, known as the XP-57. He partnered with Harry Miller to build this aircraft with a straight eight-cylinder engine, but because of slow progress on the prototype and because the idea of the engine being placed behind the pilot was already built by Bell Aircraft, the Army Air Corps let the contract lapse.

Another project that Tucker was involved with was his armored car. The Dutch government was looking for a vehicle that could handle the Dutch terrain. Tucker came up with several innovative ideas, but the armored car was his best. It could reach a speed of up to one hundred miles per hour with a rotating gun turret on top. The only problem was that the Germans invaded Holland, and that was the end of it. Tucker tried to sell his armored car to the U.S. Army, but it said that his car was too fast for combat. The military did like the rotating turret, and the navy set up a contract to build it.

Andrew Jackson Higgins, who had a government contract to build Liberty ships, purchased Tucker Aircraft. Higgins kept Tucker on as vice president of Higgins-Tucker Aviation, and together, they built the Tucker Turrets for the navy's PT boats. Initially, the turrets were produced in Tucker's machine shop. During the war, Tucker severed his partnership with Higgins, but the U.S. government confiscated the patent rights, and he fought lawsuits for years to recoup royalties on his turret.

Before the war, McAleer Manufacturing Comping made waxes and polishes for automobiles. It was awarded a government contract to produce explosives with metal materials. It purchased an old textile mill in Rochester and built bunkers for the process of the bombs produced. The bunkers were built to prevent explosions, but explosions happened, and there were deaths and injuries.

Olga Zucharuk, one of the employees, had put a note in one of the photo flash bombs (used to light up the target at night) that she packed to be sent to the front lines. The company produced over fifty thousand of these bombs, which stood four feet tall and were ten inches in diameter. These bombs were used to take aerial reconnaissance at night. They would light up the ground target 1/45 of a second—long enough to take a photograph. Zucharuk was later surprised to receive a letter from a group of airmen stationed in Guam.

15

MANHATTAN CONNECTION

The Manhattan Project was, of course, the building of the atomic bomb. There were a few people from Michigan associated with this, either by working on the project personally or witnessing its destruction in Japan. Components were manufactured at a Michigan-based food processing company's machine shop, and men from Michigan were on the ship that brought the components to the island in the Pacific. A major automotive manufacturer from Michigan helped with the refining of the uranium in Oakville, Tennessee.

Kellex Corps, a subsidiary of Kellogg's of Battle Creek, was involved in making components for the atomic bomb in its machine shop. It was believed that spies would not suspect a cereal company of making components for the atomic bomb.

"Kell" stood for "Kellogg" and "ex" for secret. The headquarters was based in the Woolworth building in Lower Manhattan. Kellex was tasked with building the equipment to process uranium. Many of the chemists who worked for Kellogg's participated in the making of the atomic bomb. Parts and supplies were produced in the machine shop in Battle Creek.

Chrysler Corp. also took part in the Manhattan Project. It built a plant in Oak Ridge, Tennessee, and helped in the refining of the uranium. Kellogg's employees, including physicists, engineers and chemists, worked on the design of the process.

According to research done by members of the Birmingham Historical Museum, a couple that was living in Birmingham, Michigan, Dr. Robert and Jane Kamm were both employed by the Army Corps of Engineers for the

Top: *Photo courtesy of the Battle Creek Historical Society.*

Bottom: The packaging process of Kellogg's cereal. *Photo courtesy of the Battle Creek Historical Society.*

Manhattan Project. Robert and Jane worked at the Los Alamos site, where the atomic bomb was developed. Robert had many skills as a metallurgical engineer, psychiatrist and theologist. Jane was head librarian and had the highest-level security clearance.

After the war, they were under constant surveillance by the U.S. government because of their knowledge of the workings of the atomic bomb. Jane was the niece of Alger Hiss, who was accused of being a Communist and a Soviet spy

Above: Dr. Robert L. Kamm and Jane Kamm photos used for their security badges. *Photo courtesy of the Los Alamos National Security Research Center.*

Left: Dr. Theron Finzel. *Photo courtesy of the Monroe Historical Museum.*

Crew members of the Enola Gay. *Photo courtesy of the National Museum of the United States Air Force.*

while working for the federal government. After a mistrial, Hiss was found guilty of two counts of perjury and sentenced to ten years in prison. He served only three and half years. Richard Nixon suspected that Jane, too, might have been a Communist. After Robert's death, Jane destroyed all the documents related to the U.S. government.

Dr. Theron Finzel, a chemical engineer and chemist from Monroe, worked for DuPont. Finzel was asked to work on the Manhattan Project and sent to Chicago, where he worked with Enrico Fermi. He later moved to Oak Ridge to process uranium. On August 6, 1945, he received a certificate from the War Department for his part in the Manhattan Project.

Two crewmembers on the Enola Gay, the plane that dropped the bomb on Hiroshima, were from Michigan: Sergeant Robert Shumard from Detroit and Staff Sergeant Wyatt Duzenbury from Mount Pleasant. They both witnessed the bombing of Hiroshima at 8:16 a.m. on April 6, 1945. The bomb killed over ninety thousand soldiers and civilians and destroyed over sixty thousand buildings.

Left: Sergeant Robert Shumard. *Right*: Staff Sergeant Wyatt Duzenbury. *Photos courtesy of the National Museum of the United States Air Force.*

Accompanying both the Enola Gay B-29 and the Bockscar B-29 that bombed Nagasaki was another B-29 bomber, Great Artiste. The pilot was Captain Frederick C. Bock from Greenville, Michigan, and the flight engineer was Master Sergeant Roderick F. Arnold from Rochester, Michigan. Their mission was to observe the effects and photograph the intensity of the bomb blasts.

There was an American soldier who was a witness on the ground at Nagasaki. Ken Rice of Michigan had joined the marines before the war. He was captured in the Philippines and endured the Bataan Death March. An estimated sixty to eighty thousand American and Filipino POWs were forced to march from Bataan, Bagac, Saysain Point, Mariveles to Camp O'Donnell, Capas, Tariac, via San Fernando, Pampanga, where the prisoners were loaded on trains. The total distance marched was between sixty and sixty-nine miles, during which 5,000 to 18,000 Filipinos and between 500 and 650 Americans died. Any POWs who fell during the march and were not helped up by their fellow POWs were executed.

Front row ground crew names are unknown. (*Back row, left to right*): Sergeant Ralph D. Curry, radio operator; Lieutenant Charles Levy, bombardier; Sergeant Robert J. Stock, tail gunner; Captain Frederick C. Bock, aircraft commander; Sergeant Ralph D. Belanger, assistant flight engineer; Lieutenant Leonard A. Godfrey, navigator; Sergeant William C. Barney, radar operator; Lieutenant Hugh C. Ferguson, copilot; Master Sergeant Roderick F. Arnold, flight engineer.

Ken Rice. *Photo courtesy of the Castle Museum.*

Ken Rice was placed on a ship destined for Japan. While en route to Japan, the ship was torpedoed by an American submarine. He survived the sinking and was picked up by another Japanese transport ship.

Rice was placed in hard labor in a coal mine until the end of the war. The coal mine was at Nagasaki. Ken was in the coal mine when the bomb was dropped. Not being above ground saved his life.

After the war, Rice remained in the marines, and during the Korean War, he was an observer on the frontlines. He retired from the marines in 1960 and became a police officer for the Saginaw Police Department. On May 25, 2019, at the age of ninety-four Sergeant Major Ken was honored in Washington, D.C., for the annual Senate Memorial Day Service.

16

THE MEN AND WOMEN
ARE COMING HOME

A fter the Japanese surrendered, our Michigan men and women came home to resume their lives as civilians. Some women went home to take care of the household, and some stayed in the factories or found jobs elsewhere. Factories began to return to prewar production of automobiles, and victory gardens went back to flower gardens. Meanwhile, many returning soldiers faced a different path to normalcy as they recovered from or adjusted to the physical and emotional damage of war.

When the Japanese signed their surrender, Captain Stuart Murray of the USS *Missouri* noticed that the ornate desk set up for the signing was too small for the documents. He ordered four sailors to find a larger table. The sailors went through the officers' quarters and found that the tables were bolted to the floor. They finally ended up in the galley, where the crew had already stowed away the tables. The sailors grabbed a table and brought it topside, where the signing was to take place. That table was produced by the Metal Office Furniture Co. of Grand Rapids, Michigan. Today, the table is with the Naval Academy Museum.

The Battle Creek Sanitarium was originally built in 1866 by Seventh-day Adventists to teach a version of holistic medicine that stressed preventative medicine. In 1876, Dr. John Harvey Kellogg purchased the hospital and expanded the building. A major part of the hospital burned down in 1902, but a new building was built in its place. Kellogg was best known for the invention of the breakfast cereal cornflakes. In the late 1920s, the hospital was in arears with the bank and went into receivership. With the outbreak of World War II, it was recommended that the building be turned into a military hospital. In 1942, the U.S. Army purchased the building and renovated it from 1,000 beds to 1,500 beds, with many new features, including ramps throughout the building.

The hospital was opened in 1943 and named after Colonel Percy L. Jones, a medical officer during the Spanish-American War. During that brief conflict, he modernized the evacuation of wounded soldiers, and during World War I, he commanded the French army ambulatory service. During World War II, patients at the Percy Jones Veterans Hospital exceeded capacity, and additional rooms were needed. W.K. Kellogg, founder of Kellogg's, had a mansion on a lake as a convalescent home that he offered to the hospital, and nearby Fort Custer supplied rooms for the overflow of patients. By the end of the war, over eleven thousand patients received treatment there. The hospital was closed for a brief period, until the Korean War, during which patients were treated for frost bite and dismemberment of limbs.

Photo courtesy of the Battle Creek Historical Society.

*Photos courtesy of the Battle
Creek Historical Society.*

Above, left: Phillip Hart. *Personal collection.*

Above, right: Bob Dole. *Photo courtesy of the Library of Congress.*

Left: Daniel Inouye. *Photo courtesy of the Library of Congress.*

It was important that during the rehabilitation, the soldiers could still do the things that they might have done before their injuries. Exercise was essential to the rehabilitation of the veterans, as was encouraging them to help themselves and to understand what they could and could not do physically and mentally. It was here in Battle Creek that the start of easements at street corners were made for the wounded who could not step up on the curb of the sidewalk.

In 2003, the building was renamed the Hart-Dole-Inouye Federal Building in honor of the three senators who served during World War II and were treated for their wounds with rehabilitation in Battle Creek. Philip Hart, from Michigan, was wounded at Normandy during the D-Day invasion. Bob Dole, from Kansas, was wounded over Italy, and Daniel Inouye, from Hawaii, was wounded in combat in Italy. These men met each other at the hospital and promised to go into public service after the war.

Many of the factories that produced war materials are gone today to make way for newer and more automated factories. Some are preserved as museums, and others are repurposed. Many of the greatest generation are passing away every day, and their stories are being recorded before they pass on by people who care. Let us remember them and honor them.

APPENDIX

The following is a list of Michigan manufactures and what they produced before and during the war. This list was compiled by the Heritage Research Center, Ltd. Note that the boat and ship builders are not listed. That list is provided in chapter 3.

City	Manufacturer	Products	During the War
Adrian	Bohn Aluminum and Brass Corp	New plant	Extruded aluminum alloy shapes, bars, rods and magnesium castings
Albion	Albion Malleable Iron Co.	Foundry Products	Malleable iron castings
Albion	Union Steel Products Co.	Wire Products	Depth bombs and torpedo parts
Allegan	Standard Steel Spring Co. Blood Brothers Machine Co.	Auto parts	Propeller shafts and universal joints
Almont	Hurd Lock and Mfg. Co.	Hardware	Primers, 5 inches
Alpena	Besser Mfg. Co.	Concrete mixers	Concrete black machinery

City	Manufacturer	Products	During the War
Ann Arbor	American Broach Machine Co.	Broaching tools	Broaching tools
Ann Arbor	Argus Inc.	Photographic equipment	Optical Apparatus and lens, telescopes and gunsights
Ann Arbor	International Ind. Inc.	Optical elements for binoculars	Optical elements for binoculars
Ann Arbor	Sunstrand Machine Tool Co.	Machine tools	Broaching machines
Battle Creek	Duplex Printing Press Co.	Printing machinery and parts	Gun carriages and mounts 37mm
Battle Creek	Eaton Mfg. Co. Wilcox Rich Divsion	Aircraft intake and exhaust valves	Aircraft intake and exhaust valves
Bay City	Dow Chemical Co.	Nonferrous metal	Magnesium sand castings and magnesium metal fabrications
Bay City	Electric Auto Lite Co.	Automobile parts	Gyro indicators, automatic gyro pilots A-5, automatic pilots mark IV, directional gyro pilots
Bay City	Kuhlman Electric Co.	Radar equipment, bomb sticks and mine containers	Radar equipment, bomb sticks and mine containers
Bay City	Smalley General Co.	Machine tools	Thread milling machines
Benton Harbor	Dnx Engine Co. See: Hercules Motors Corp., Dachel-Carter Shipbuilding Corp.	Shipbuilding and repair	Subchasers, 136 feet, motor driven minesweepers, rescue tugs

City	Manufacturer	Products	During the War
Benton Harbor	Niles Steel Products See: Republic Steel Corp, Nineteen Hundred Corp.	Fuzes, m-48 a2	Fuzes, m-48 a2
Benton Harbor	Ross Carrier Co.	Construction machinery Industrial cars and trucks	
Big Rapids	Hanchett Mfg. Co.	Machine tools	Flat surface grinding machines
Bronson	Darling LA Co.	Shelving	Gun mounts
Buchanan	Clark Equipment Co.	High speed drills	High speed drills, reamers
Buchanan	Clark Truck Tractor Div.	Reamers and countersinks	Reamers and countersinks
Capac	Capac Mfg.	Plastic products	Helmet liners
Center Line	Westinghouse Electric and Mfg. Co.	New plant	Machine guns and parts 20mm
Chelsea	Federal Screw Works	Bolts, nuts, washers and rivets	Projectiles, fuses, boosters and screw machine products
Dearborn	Ford Motor Co., Rouge Plant	Automobiles	Aircraft engines and parts, engines for trucks and tanks, tank parts, universal gun carrier parts, gun mounts 75mm
Dearborn	Ford Motor Co., Tire Plant	Aircraft Parts	Aircraft parts
Dearborn	Graham Paige Motor Co.	Cars and parts	Aircraft connecting rods
Dearborn	Hydraulic Machinery Inc.	Industrial machinery	Cranes

City	Manufacturer	Products	During the War
Detroit	Aeronautical Products Inc.	Aircraft and parts	Aircraft engine shafts, stems, bushings, valves, et cetera
Detroit	Allied Chemical and Dye Corp.	Oven coke	Carbon pitch, Napthalene, 78c, phenol and cresols, 74c CMP crude solvents
Detroit	American Metal Products Co.	Wrought pipes	Axil housings, nacelles, engine mounts B-24
Detroit	American Radiator and Standard Sanitary Corp. American Blower Corp.	Hydraulic couplings for fluid drivers and marine blowers	Hydraulic coupling for fluid and marine blowers
Detroit	Apex Broach Co.	Machine tools	Broaching tools
Detroit	Arrow Tool and Reamer Co.	Machine tools	Reamers
Detroit	Asam Mfg. Co.	Machine tool parts	Machine tool parts
Detroit	Bower Roller Bearing Co.	Pumps and pumping equipment	Crankshaft roller equipment bearings for aircraft engines
Detroit	Briggs Mfg. Co.	Automobile engines	Aircraft parts for many different planes, truck cabs and tops tank hulls, tools and dies and aircraft gun turrets
Detroit	Budd Wheel Co.	Truck wheels	Rocket fuzes, 115mm shells, truck wheels and brake drums
Detroit	Bundy Tubing Co.	Tank tread tubing aircraft tubing	Tank tread tubing, aircraft tubing and glider tubing
Detroit	Burroughs Adding Machines	Office and store	Norton bombsights m-9

City	Manufacturer	Products	During the War
Detroit	Cabot Carbon Co.	Thread ring gauges and thread plug gauges	Thread ring gauges and thread plug gauges
Detroit	Castoloy Corp.	Machine tools	Tools, dies, jigs, fixtures and special patented corrosend tools for aircraft
Detroit	Champion Spark Plug Co.	Spark plugs	Aircraft and tank spark plugs, other spark plugs and insulators for spark plugs
Detroit	Chicago Pneumatic Tools Co.	Pneumatic hydraulics and electric tools	Pneumatic hydraulic and electric tools
Detroit	Chrysler, Jefferson Plant	Automobile engines	Multi-bank tank motors, anti-aircraft guns 40mm
Detroit	Chrysler Corp. Kercheval Plant	Automobiles and Equipment	Anti-aircraft guns, 40mm marine tractors, aircraft parts, engines and turbines
Detroit	Colman Frederick and Ons Inc.	Jigs, tools and fixtures	Jigs, tools and fixtures
Detroit	Colonial Broach Co.	Machine tools	Broaching machines
Detroit	Continental Die Casting Co.	Nonferrous metal	Shot 3.0-inch AP, rockets 4.5-inch T-22 and T-46
Detroit	Continental Motors	Aircraft parts	Tank engines, aircraft engines R-975 combat vehicle motors
Detroit	Cross Gear and machine Co.	Machine tools	Milling, boring, gear chambering and burning machine
Detroit	Dalzen Tool and Mfg.	Machine tools	Thread grinders, ground thread taps, special tools
Detroit	Detroit Branch Co. Inc.	Machine tools	Broaching tools

City	Manufacturer	Products	During the War
Detroit	Detroit Brass Co Inc.	Boosters	Boosters and Malleable Works
Detroit	Detroit Cutboard Products Corp.	Tank track end connectors	Tank track end connectors
Detroit	Detroit Diesel Engine Division	Engines and turbines	Marine diesels and spare parts tank diesels
Detroit	Detroit Gear Aircraft Parts Division	Automobile parts	Aircraft valve tappets, guides, rollers and pistons parts
Detroit	Detroit Gear Machine Division	Automobile parts	Synchronized reverse transmission marine reduction gears, oil and water pumps, motor truck transmission, service transmission
Detroit	Detroit Harvester Co.	Machine shop	Aircraft engine parts products
Detroit	Detroit Lubricator Co. See American Radiator and Standard Sanitary, Detroit Michigan Stove Co.	Heating Apparatus	Armor plate
Detroit	Detroit Reamer and Tool Co.	Machine tools	Drills, high-speed reamers and special cutters
Detroit	Detroit Transmission Division	Automobile Transmissions	Hydraulics transmissions armored cars, tanks and torqmatic transmissions for tanks
Detroit	Detroit Universal Duplicator Corp.	Machine tool controls	Machine tool controls
Detroit	Differential Wheel Corp.	Automobile equipment	Tank bogie wheels, differential dual wheels, tank support roller

City	Manufacturer	Products	During the War
Detroit	Dodge Forge Plant	Anti-aircraft guns 40mm, aluminum alloy forgings	Anti-aircraft guns 40 mm aluminum alloy forgings
Detroit	Eaton Mfg. Co., Spring Division	Volute springs for track suspension assembly	Volute springs for track suspension assembly
Detroit	Eclipse Counterbore Co.	Machine tools	Cutting tools
Detroit	Eureka Vacuum Cleaner Co.	Electrical appliances	Training gas masks, noncombatant mask
Detroit	Ex-cell-o Corp	Machine tools	Nozzle plates for rockets, boring machines, thread, grinders, center lapping machines, et cetera
Detroit	Fargo Motor Corp.	Containers for military vehicles	Containers for military vehicles
Detroit	Federal Mogul Corp.	Nonferrous metal products	Aircraft engine valves, bearing cam rings, oil seal parts, marine propellers, et cetera
Detroit	Fisher Body Division	Automobiles	Aircraft sections, gun breach housings and gun mounts
Detroit	Ford Motor Co., Lincoln Plant	Automobiles	Tank engines
Detroit	Gemmer Mfg. Co.	Automobile parts	Gun turret forms, shot 40mm, steering gear assemblies, worm gears for turret
Detroit	General Electric Co.	Electrical appliances	Tungsten carbide cores for 3-inch shot
Detroit	General Motors Cadillac Division	Automobiles	Medium tanks

City	Manufacturer	Products	During the War
Detroit	Graf V I, Co.	Aircraft fittings	Aircraft fittings
Detroit	Graham Paige Motor Co.	Automotive parts	Articulating rods, connecting rods and cylinders heads
Detroit	Greenfield Tab	Machine tools	Ground thread high speed taps
Detroit	Holley Carburetor Co.	Carburetors	Fuzes, Aircraft engine carburetors
Detroit	Huck Mfg. Co.	Aluminum and more rivets	Aluminum and more rivets
Detroit	Hudson Motor Car	Automobiles and parts	Aircraft assembles, marine engines, shells 37mm
Detroit	Hupp Motor Car Co.	Automobiles	Base plugs for bombs and tank components
Detroit	Jacobs Aircraft Engine Co.	Aircraft engines	Amphibious tank tracks, volute spring suspensions, M4 tanks
Detroit	Kelsey-Hayes Wheel Co.	Automobile parts	Road wheel assembly parts, track supporting roller parts, tank parts, shells 3-inch aa, 4-inch HC
Detroit	Long Mfg. Division	Automobile equipment	Ordnance material
Detroit	Lyon Inc.	40mm cartridge cases	40mm cartridge cases
Detroit	McCord Corp	Automobile equipment	Rifle shell bodies, bomb suspension bands, steel helmets, link loading machines and auto parts
Detroit	McLaren Screw Products Co.	Screw machine products	Fuzes

City	Manufacturer	Products	During the War
Detroit	Michigan Die Casting Co.	Wrought pipe, nonferrous metal products	Steel castings, seamless steel tubing for aircraft nose cone worm gears, machine tools
Detroit	Micromatic Hone Corp.	Machine tools	Honing machines, tools, fixtures, cutting tools and parts
Detroit	Midwest Tool and Mfg. Co.	Machine tools	Metal cutting tools
Detroit	Motor Products Corp.	Automobile parts	Rear gun turrets B-24, cartridge, cases 20mm bushings for tank suspensions, military vehicles parts
Detroit	Motor Tool Mfg. Co.	Machine tools	Metal cutting tools
Detroit	Murchey Machine and Tool	Machine tools	Machine tools, small tools, chasers and parts
Detroit	Murray Corp. of America	Automobile parts	Aircraft wings, nacelles, ailerons, sub-assemblies, search lights, military chassis frames, gun turrets
Detroit	Nash-Kelvinator Corp.	Refrigerators and Electrical appliance	Helicopters R-6, aircraft propellers, propeller governors, bomb fuses, chemical bombs m74
Detroit	National Tool Salvage Co.	Machine shop repairs	Salvage of tools and cutters
Detroit	National Twist Drill and Tool Co.	Machine tools	Milling cutters and reamers
Detroit	Packard Motor Car Co.	Automobiles	Marine engines (PT boats), spare parts, aircraft engines, aluminum castings
Detroit	Palmer-Bee Co. Ellettsville Inc.	Conveyors	Radar equipment, shells 75mm

City	Manufacturer	Products	During the War
Detroit	Parker Wolverine Co.	Steel cups for 45 cal.	Steel cups for 45 cal. bullet jacket
Detroit	Plymouth Plant	Automobiles	Landing gears, anti-aircraft guns 40mm
Detroit	Plymouth Steel Co	Cold drawn alloy bar steel	Cold drawn allow bar steel
Detroit	Putman Tool Co.	Machine tools	Metal cutting tools
Detroit	Rafco Tool and Mfg. Co.	Ordnance materials	Ordnance materials
Detroit	Redford Tool and Die Co.	Tools	Automatic aircraft cannon parts 20mm
Detroit	Republic Aircraft, Products Division	Airplanes and parts	Aircraft engine tappets guides, valve locks, seats and aircraft engine parts
Detroit	Revere Copper	Sheets, strips and bands	Cartridge cases and cups
Detroit	Rotary Electric Steel Co.	Steel works	Hot metal for electric furnaces
Detroit	S and S Tool and Mfg. Co.	Machine tools	Gun, tank and airplane parts
Detroit	Sal Way Steel Treating Co.	Heat treating of cutting tools and small parts	Heat treating of cutting tools and small parts
Detroit	Shatterproof Glass Co.	Glass products	Broaches
Detroit	Sherwood Brass Works	Brass products	Water pumps and parts
Detroit	Sperry Corp. Vickers Inc.	Hydraulic equipment	Hydraulic equipment
Detroit	Standard Tube Co.	Wrought pipes	Shell forgings, ammunition shells, welded steel tubing, tank tread tubing
Detroit	Steel Materials Corp.	Steel cartridge cases 20mm	Steel cartridge cases 20mm

City	Manufacturer	Products	During the War
Detroit	Ternsteot, Mfg. Divsion	Horizontal gyros, vertical gyros, remote compasses	Horizontal gyros, vertical gyros, remote compasses
Detroit	Timbeam Inc.	Laminated wood	Laminated wood
Detroit	Timkin Detroit Axle Co.	Axles and Transmissions	Axles, transfer cases, service parts for military and commercial trucks
Detroit	Tompkins Printing Equipment Co.	Aircraft cup screws, bolts and turn buckles screw machine products	Aircraft transfer cases, bolts and turn buckles screw machine products
Detroit	Tungsten Carbice Tool Co.	Machine tools	Hard alloyed production tools
Detroit	United Drill and Tool Co.	Twist drills, reamers countersinks, counterbores and special cutting tools	Twist drills, reamers, countersinks, counterbores and special cutting tools
Detroit	U.S. Broach Co.	Machine tools	Broaches, reamers, form tools
Detroit	U.S. Rubber Co.	Rubber products	Plastic steering wheels, rubber cement, self-sealing fuel cells, tire flaps, aircraft engine mountings
Detroit	Vinco Corp.	Machine tools	Hardened and ground tools and gauges, high precision checking and production instruments and special machinery
Detroit	Welch Industries Inc.	Machine tools	Milling cutters, reamers, drills, flat, circular and drove-tail form tools

City	Manufacturer	Products	During the War
Detroit	Wolverine Tube Co.	Alloying	Condenser tools
Detroit	Woodall Industries Inc.	Paper products	Landing gear doors B-26, aft fuselage sections F4U-1
Detroit	Young LA Spring & Wire Co.	Projectiles, gun parts and shells	Projectiles, gun parts and shells
Domagiac	Ruby Furnace Co.	Furnaces	Ammunition box liners, bomb parts
Ecorse	Bowen Products Corp.	Automobile stampings	Fuse parts, cartridge cases, cups coined and smoke shells
Fenton	Genesee Tool Co.	Cutting tools and gun parts	Cutting tools and gun parts
Ferndale	Reichel Lass Inc. See American Home Products Corp., Reichel Chemical Corp	New plant	Chemical and resins
Ferndale	Wesson Tools Co.	Machine tools	High speed and carbide tipping cutting tools
Ferndale	Woodworth NA Co.	Aircraft and parts	Ring and plug type gauges, taps, Form tools, precision aircraft engine parts, gear pinions, shell sleeves, propeller shafts, screws
Flint	Air Reduction Sales Co.	Oxygen	Oxygen
Flint	Flint Trolley Coach Inc.	Trolleys	Motor vehicle transportation
Flint	GM, AC Spark Plug Division	Spark plugs	Automatic pilots, computators, gunsights, bomb sites, fuel pumps, aircraft spark plugs and bearings

City	Manufacturer	Products	During the War
Flint	GM, Buick Motor Division	Automobiles and parts	Tank destroyers, automobile cylinder heads, truck parts, motor carriers, aluminum gas, cylinder heads, engine blocks and automobile fenders
Flint	GM, Chevrolet Motor Division	Automobile parts	Guns 90mm, gun tubes spares 90mm and M1 and M2 and armored cars
Flint	GM, Fisher Body Division	Automobiles	Medium tanks, tank transmission, motor gun cartridges
Frankenmuth	Universal Engineering Products	Bushing	Bushing
Grand Haven	Allen Calculators Inc.	Office machines	Bank and turn indicators C1, turn control for A5 automatic pilots, electronic turbo supercharger regulators
Grand Haven	Ashby Drilling Co.	Oil and brine well drilling	Oil, gas and brine well drilling
Grand Haven	Camfield Mfg. Co.	Plywood	Compreg wood propellers
Grand Rapids	American Seating Co.	Public building furniture	Spars, caps, outer wing panels, aircraft seats B-26
Grand Rapids	Berkey and Gay Furniture Co.	Household furniture	Wooden sections and parts for aircraft
Grand Rapids	Doehler-Jarvis Corp	Hardware	Electro chromium plating of 50-caliber machine gun barrels
Grand Rapids	Extruded Metals Inc.	Brass billets and brass rods, extruded aluminum alloys	Brass billets and brass rods, extruded aluminum alloys

City	Manufacturer	Products	During the War
Grand Rapids	Fisher Body Division	Breech housings, shells and gun mounts	Breech housings, shells and gun mounts
Grand Rapids	Grand Rapids Brass Co.	Hardware	Hardware
Grand Rapids	Haskelite Mfg. Corp.	Steel metal work	Duramold process aircraft and sub-assembly
Grand Rapids	Irwin-Pederson Arms Co.	Carbines	Carbines
Grand Rapids	Lear Inc.	Aircraft actuators, Electric motors and gear boxes	Aircraft actuators, electric motors and gear boxes
Grand Rapids	McInerney Spring and Wire Co.	Wire products	Fragmentation bombs and rocket motors
Grand Rapids	Michigan Gas Transmission Corp.	Magnesium and castings	Magnesium and castings
Grand Rapids	Nash Kelvinator Corp.	Refrigerators	Aircraft parts and helicopters R-6
Grandville	Winters and Crampton Corp.	Hardware	Projectiles 40mm, capacitors, ammunitions boxes, heat treating struts, sub-assemblies, heat treating baffles
Greenville	Federal Mogul Corp.	Bronze propeller castings, marine propellers	Bronze propeller castings, marine propellers
Greenville	Gibson Refrigerator Co.	Refrigerators	Waco gliders
Hamtramck	Chrysler Corp., Dodge Bros. Main Plant	Automobiles and equipment, metal working equipment	Gyro compasses mark xiv, aluminum castings, antiaircraft guns 40mm, aluminum forgings radar components

City	Manufacturer	Products	During the War
Hamtramck	Detroit Tap and Tool Co.	Machine tools	Ground form taps, gauges, hubs, cutting tools, marine engine gears
Hamtramck	Gear Grinding Machine Co.	Machine tools	Unknown
Hartford	Burnett Casting Co.	Aluminum castings	Aluminum castings
Hastings	Hastings Mfg. Co.	Auto accessories	Aircraft engine piston rings, projectiles 40mm, 20mm and cartridge clips
Highland Park	Ex-cell-o Corp	New plant	Aircraft engine parts
Highland Park	Ford Motor Co.	Automobiles and parts	M-4 tanks, anti-aircraft guns 40mm, military trucks, aircraft engines, B-29 nose, and center fuselage
Hillsdale	Allied Products Corp.	Machine tools	Aircraft engine parts, gun breech slides
Hillsdale	Paramount Mfg. Co. Inc.	Aircraft nuts, studs, et cetera	Aircraft nuts, studs, et cetera
Holland	Fafnir Bearing Co.	Ball bearings	Ball bearings
Holland	Hart and Cooley Mfg. Co.	Heating apparatus	Wrought steel products, shell bodies 60mm
Ionia	Ypsilanti Read Furniture Co.	Household furniture	Jeep seats, civilian bodies, tarpaulins receiver covers, gun mount covers and jungle hammocks
Iron Mountain	Ford Charcoal Co.	Charcoal	Waco CG-4A and YCG-13 gliders
Jackson	Aeroquip Corp	Couplings and hose assemblies	Couplings and hose assemblies
Jackson	Ampco Twist Drill Co.	Machine tools	High-speed tapered and straight shank drills

City	Manufacturer	Products	During the War
Jackson	Goodyear Michigan Corp.	Rubber products	Anti-tank guns 3 inch
Jackson	Hancock Mfg. Co.	Hardware	Gun parts, anti-aircraft gun parts, tank parts, aircraft parts, projectiles, jackets and cartridges and anti-tank mines
Jackson	Houdaille Hetshey Corp.	Automotive parts	Bombs, 500 pounds
Jackson	Miller McCluskey Plating Co.	Electric plating combat vehicle parts	Electric plating combat vehicle parts
Jackson	Muskegon Motor Specialties Co.	Crankshafts	Tank track pins
Kalamazoo	Borg-Warner	Transmission parts	Amphibious tanks
Kalamazoo	Fuller Mfg. Co.	Heavy-duty truck transmissions	Heavy-duty truck transmissions
Lansing	GM, Olds Motor Division	Truck axle forgings	Guns for aircraft, projectiles, shells rocket assembly
Lansing	Lansing Drop Forge Co.	Iron and steel forgings	Tail cones for 81mm illuminating shells
Lansing	Lansing Paint and Color Co.	Paint and varnishes	Ammonium picrate
Lansing	Nash-Kelvinator Corp.	Automobiles	Hydromatic Dural 3-blade
Lansing	REO Motor Inc.	Automobiles	Armored cars, military trucks, bomb fuzer axel sets, 2½ ton transmissions
Lincoln Park	Lincoln Park Tool and Gauges Co.	Engines turbines	Gauges
Ludington	Dow Chemical Co.	Drilling magnesium salt wells	Drilling magnesium salt wells

City	Manufacturer	Products	During the War
Ludington	Dow Magnesium Corp.	New plant	Magnesium chloride cell feed
Manchester	Ford Motor Co.	Rate of climb indicators	Rate of climb indicators
Marshall	Eaton Mfg. Co., Wilcox Rich Division	Aircraft engine bolts, Screws, lubricating and cooling pumps for tanks, auto and truck engine valves	Aircraft engine bolts, screws lubricating and cooling pumps for auto and truck engine valves
Marysville	Dow Magnesium Corp.	New plant	Magnesium metal and alloys
Melvindale	Timken Detroit Axle Co.	New plant	Axle and gear forgings
Midland	Dow Chemical Co.	Aluminum products, electrical equipment industrial chemicals	Aniline oil, phenol, bromine, monochlorbenzol, salicylic acid, ethylene gas, ethyl benzene, parachlorphenol, ethyl cellulose, monochloracetic acid, metal alloy forgings
Midland	Kerotest Mfg. Co.	Reaction chamber for recoil mortar	Reaction chamber for recoil mortar
Monroe	Aluminum Co. of America	New plant	Forged aluminum cylinder heads, scalped ingots
Monroe	Lay-Z-Boy	Furniture	Seats for tanks, jeeps and others
Monroe	Monroe Auto Equipment Co.	Automobile parts	Shot, 37MM, AP
Muskegon	Agerstrand Corp.	Special machinery, steel treating	Gauges, jigs and special machinery

City	Manufacturer	Products	During the War
Muskegon	Brunswick-Balke-Callender Co.	Assembly plants for aircraft	Assembly plants for aircraft
Muskegon	Continental Aviation Engineering Co.	Aircraft engines	Aircraft engines R 134, I 1430, V1650-3
Muskegon	Continental Motor Corp.	Engines and turbines	Tank engines
Muskegon	Kayden Engineering Corp.	Power transmission and engines	Roller-bearing gun mounts 40 mm, airplanes, assault boats parachutes, flares, gliders, power transmissions
Muskegon	Lakey Foundry	Foundry products	Iron and steel castings for guns and tanks, cylinder blocks and heads, and manifold castings
Muskegon	Muskegon Motor Specialties Co.	Camshafts for aircraft and other internal combustions engines	Camshafts for aircraft and other internal combustions engines
Muskegon	Muskegon Piston Ring Co.	Piston Rings	Aircraft engine piston rings
Muskegon	Peoples Transport Co.	Automobiles	Automobiles
Muskegon	Sealed Power Corp.	Pistons and pistons rings	Piston rings for aircraft and other vehicles, piston and cylinder sleeves
Muskegon	West Michigan Steel Foundry Co.	Foundry products	Gun mount castings 20mm
Rochester	McAlear Mfg. Co.	Atomized aluminum powder	Atomized aluminum powder, parachute flares, trip flares and photo flash bombs
Royal Oak	Sperry Corp, Vickers Inc.	New plant	Hydraulic equipment for gun turrets

City	Manufacturer	Products	During the War
Saginaw	Eaton Mfg Co.	Machine shop products	Aircraft valves, seats, screws, flyweights, bolts, et cetera
Saginaw	Saginaw Steering, GM Division	Steering gears	Machine guns, carbines, M1 and parts and cansine receivers
Saginaw	Wickes Boiler Co.	Heating apparatus	Boiler drums, boilers and boiler drumheads
Saginaw	Wickes Bros.	Machine tools	Single and double end borings mills, gun turning and boring lathes, shell turning and engine crankshaft turn lathes
Sebawiang	Aircraft Industries Inc.	Automotive replacement parts	Automotive replacement parts
St. Joseph	Auto Specialties Mfg. Co.	Foundry products	Shells, shot, lifting jacks hydraulic and mechanical
St Louis	Michigan Chemical Corp.	Industrial chemicals	Dead burned magnesite and periclose
Tecumseh	Tecumseh Products Co.	Refrigeration equipment	20mm and 40mm projectiles
Three River	Fairbanks Morse and Co.	Diesel engine propulsion unit	Diesel engine propulsion unit
Traverse City	Cherry Growers Inc.	Preserved foods	Food processing
Trenton	Boeckeler Associates Co.	Ethyl alcohol	Ethyl alcohol 190 proof
Trenton	Trenton Valley Distillers Corp.	Distilling industrial alcohol	Distilling industrial alcohol
Utica	Packard Proving Ground	Repair and testing combat vehicles	Repair and testing combat vehicles

City	Manufacturer	Products	During the War
Warren	American Cutter and Engineering Corp.	Drills, reamers, milling cutters and counter bores	Drills, reamers, milling cutters and counter bores
Warren	Chrysler Corporation, Desoto Plant (Detroit Tank Aresnal)	New plant	Anti-aircraft guns, gun mount mechanism assemblies, medium tank transmissions and drive assemblies
Warren	Super Tool Co.	Machine tools	Tungsten carbide–tipped cutting tools
Wayne	Bendix Products, Aircraft Division	New plant	Aircraft carburetors, Weiss universal joints
Wayne	Consolidated Vultee Aircraft Corp. (formerly Stinson)	Airplanes	Airplanes AT-19 Reliant and L-5 Sentinel
Ypsilanti	Central Specialty Co.	Foundry products	Gun mounts
Ypsilanti	Ford Motor Co.	Automotive electrical equipment	Motor generators, tractor trailer sub-assemblies
Ypsilanti	Motor State Products Co.	Automobiles parts	Folding top assemblies for scout cars, tank parts, gun buffers
Ypsilanti	Willow Run Bomber Factory	New plant	Heavy bombers, B-24 Liberators and sub-assemblies

BIBLIOGRAPHY

Print

Arbic, Bernie, and Nancy Steinhaus. *Upbound Downbound: The Story of the Soo Locks*. New York: Priscilla Press Allegan Forest, 2005.

Chabot, Larry. *The U.P. Goes to War: Upper Michigan and Its Heroes of World War II*. Marquette, MI: North Harbor Publishing, 2006.

Clive, Alan. *State of War Michigan in World War II*. Ann Arbor: University of Michigan Press, 1979.

Davis, Michael W.R. *Detroit's Wartime Industry Arsenal of Democracy*. Charleston, SC: Arcadia Publishing, 2007.

Dempsey, Dave. *William G. Milliken Michigan's Passionate Moderate*. Ann Arbor: University of Michigan Press, 2006.

Fornes, Mike. *USCGC WAGB83 Mackinaw: An Illustrated History of a Great Lakes Queen*. Cheboygan, MI: Cheboygan Tribune Printing, 2005.

Haltiner, Robert E. *The Town That Went to War*. Alpena, MI: Model Printing Service, 2001.

Heaton, Dan. "Over Here, Over Here: Michigan's Fort's and Airfields." *Michigan History*, November/December 2018.

Kowalski, Greg. *Hamtramck the World War II Years*. Charleston, SC: Arcadia Publishing, 2007.

Larson, Deborah J. *Home Town Rochester*. Rochester, MI: Rochester-Avon Historical Society, 2008.

Lee, James. "Brits Invade Grosse Ile." *Special Today: Heritage*, May 30, 1993.

Lewis, Norma, and Christine Nyholm. *Muskegon*. Charleston, SC: Arcadia Publishing, 2018.

Pauley, Robert F. *Images of Aviation: Michigan Aircraft Manufacturers*. Charleston, SC: Arcadia Publishing, 2009.

Ranville, Judy, and Nancy Campbell. *Memories of Mackinaw*. Petoskey, MI: Little Traverse Printing, 1976.

Rickman, Sarah Byrn. *Nancy Love and the WASP Ferry Pilots of World War II*. Denton: University of North Texas Press, 2008.

———. *The Originals: The Women's Auxiliary Ferrying Squadron of World War II*. Sarasota, FL: Disc-Us Books, 2001.

Schirado, Richard H.J. *Rockford*. Charleston, SC: Arcadia Publishing, 2009.

Soule, Michael D. "The Unit History of the 107th Tactical Reconnaissance Squadron, Michigan Air National Guard." Air Command and Staff College Air University, Maxwell AFB AL, April 1978.

Stevens, Deidre. "When World War II Came to the Strait." *Michigan History*, March/April 2013.

Young, Coleman, and Lonnie Wheeler. *Hard Stuff: The Autobiography of Mayor Coleman Young*. New York: Penguin, 1994.

Websites

Bowman, Craig. "When the Japanese Bombed North Dorr, Michigan." War History Online. February 26, 2017. https://www.warhistoryonline.com.

Burck, Dennis. "Farmington Bombed in WWLL? The Japanese Balloon Bomb Incident of 1945." *Farmington Voice*, June 3, 2018. https://farmingtonvoice.com.

Hodgson, Lynn Philip. "Canada's Historic Jewel Faces the Wrecking Ball." Camp-X. http://www.camp-x.com.

National Museum United States Army. "254th Engineer Combat Battalion." Army Historical Foundation. https://armyhistory.org.

Pepin, John. "Viewer's Guide: The Enemy in Our Midst." PBS. https://d1qbemlbhjecig.cloudfront.net.

Rare Historical Photos. "Henry Ford Receiving the Grand Cross of the German Eagle from Nazi Officials, 1938." https://rarehistoricalphotos.com.

Suhs, Mardi. "Chris-Craft Cadillac Produced the Landing Craft for D-Day." *Cadillac News*, June 6, 2018. https://www.cadillacnews.com.

Film

Pepin, John. *The Enemy in Our Midst: Nazi Prisoner of War Camps in Michigan's Upper Peninsula*. WNMU 13 TV, Marquette, 2004.

ABOUT THE AUTHOR

Daniel W. Mason studied history at Lake Superior College in the early 1980s and always had a passion for history. He now works full time for an overnight carrier as a tractor-trailer driver and published his first history book, *Images in Aviation: Detroit Metro Airport,* in 2011. He volunteers his time to digitize photos for the Wayne County Airport Authority. He documents and takes photos of events at Detroit Metropolitan Airport in his spare time and answers any questions on the airport's history. Daniel also helped with the timeline history of the Detroit Metro Airport website.

Daniel tries to promote the history of the WASP who served at Detroit Metro Airport during World War II and promotes the history in local communities. He is president of the Detroit Metro Airport Historical Society and president of the Downriver Historical Organization.